Duckworth Overlook

Why Won't You Apologize?

"If you want to know why Harriet Lerner is one of my great heroes, *Why Won't You Apologize?* is the answer. This book is a game changer."

—Brené Brown, author of the
#1 *New York Times* bestseller *Rising Strong*

"Harriet Lerner is one hell of a wise woman. She draws you in with deft and engaging prose, and then changes your life with her rigorous intelligence and her deeply human advice. I promise that you will never see 'the apology' in quite the same way."

—Esther Perel, MA, LMFT,
author of *Mating in Captivity*

"If you want to learn the art and craft of apology and repair when you've hurt someone, this is your book. If you are frustrated with a person who is no good at accepting responsibility for hurting you, this is your book. If you want powerful insights into human relationships, let me say it plainly: *This is the best self-help book I've ever read!*"

—William Doherty, Ph.D., professor of
Family Social Science at the University of Minnesota,
author of *Take Back Your Marriage*

"*Why Won't You Apologize?* is at once practical and profound. It guides us through the most difficult places in human relationships. Read this book, then pass it on to the non-apologizer in your life."

—Monica McGoldrick, MA, LCSW, Ph.D. (Honorary),
director of the Multicultural Family Institute in
Highland Park, New Jersey

"With luminous stories and clinical nuance, Harriet Lerner shows us the value and power of apologies—and how to deliver and receive them. We applaud her achievement, including her compelling analysis of the dynamics of forgiveness. We recommend this book to anyone who has suffered hurt from others or caused others to suffer. Who among us has not done both?"

elly Hunt, Ph.D.,
 the Love You Want

"With her signature punch and humor, Harriet Lerner tackles the injuries that occur in marriage, family, and friendship. Her advice for repairing hurts and earning forgiveness is fresh, profound, life-affirming, and immediately useful."

—Janis Abrahms Spring, Ph.D., author of
After the Affair and *How Can I Forgive You?*

"A profoundly insightful look into the many ways humans hurt each other and the power of apology to restore broken relationships. Harriet Lerner has written a valuable guide for both those who deserve an apology and those who owe one."

—John Kador, author of *Effective Apology*

"I love Harriet Lerner's work!"

—Anne Lamott, author of *Help, Thanks, Wow*

"Lerner takes us beyond the simple 'I'm sorry' to show us how to restore connection with those we love the most. This wise and eminently down-to-earth book is a guide that will last a lifetime and heal the hearts of so many."

—Dr. Sue Johnson, author of *Hold Me Tight* and *Love Sense*

"*Why Won't You Apologize?* is an immensely intelligent book. Lerner is an intrepid agent of change. What a gift!"

—Judith V. Jordan, Ph.D., director of the Jean Baker Miller Training Institute at the Wellesley Center for Women

Praise for *The Dance of Anger*

"A careful and compassionate exploration of women's anger"

— Susie Orbach, author of *In Therapy*

"Of all the books that have been written about the personal relationships of women and what to do about them, this is the most sound. Like a family heirloom, it can be passed from generation to generation as it is based on profound and lasting truths"

— Peggy Papp, M.S.W.,
The Ackerman Institute for Family Therapy

Why Won't You Apologize?

Why Won't You Apologize?

*HEALING BIG BETRAYALS
AND EVERYDAY HURTS*

Harriet Lerner

Duckworth Overlook

First published in 2017 by Duckworth Overlook

LONDON
30 Calvin Street, London E1 6NW
T: 020 7490 7300
E: info@duckworth-publishers.co.uk
www.ducknet.co.uk
For bulk and special sales please contact sales@duckworth-publishers.co.uk

First published in the United States by Touchstone,
an imprint of Simon & Schuster, Inc., New York

A catalogue record for this book is available from the British Library

9780715651582

13 5 7 9 10 8 6 4 2

Printed and bound in Great Britain by Clays Ltd, St Ives plc

For my grandchildren

Cyrus and Theo
Lucía and Marcela

And for their parents

Matt and Jo
Ben and Ari

Contents

CHAPTER 1

The Many Faces of "I'm Sorry"

My humorist friend Jennifer Berman drew a cartoon of the "guy with a million excuses." My personal favorite is, "I'm sorry . . . but you never ASKED me if I was married with kids." Then there's the *New Yorker* cartoon that shows a father talking to his grown son. "I wanted to be there for you growing up, I really did," the dad says. "But I got a foot cramp. And then a thing came up at the store—anyway, you understand."

While the humor of both cartoons rests on their absurdity, we have all received apologies followed by rationalizations that undo them. They are never satisfying. In fact, they do considerable harm.

I've been studying apologies—and the men and women who can't give them—for over two decades. Of course, you don't need to be an expert on the subject to recognize when a well-deserved apology is not forthcoming, or when a bad apology flattens you. "I'm sorry" won't cut it if it's insincere, a quick way to get out of a difficult conversation, or followed by a justification or excuse.

The healing power of a *good* apology is also immediately recognizable. When someone offers me a genuine apology, I feel relieved and soothed. Whatever anger and resentment I may still be harboring melts away. I also feel better when I offer an apology I know is due. I'm enormously grateful that I can repair the disconnection after having made a mistake or acted badly. Not that I've always been a champion apologizer. With my husband, Steve, for example, I like to apologize for exactly my share of the problem—as I calculate it, of course—and I expect him to apologize for his share, also as I calculate it. Needless to say, we don't always do the same maths.

We're all apology-challenged with certain people and in some situations. Some apologies are easier to offer than others. It's one thing to forget to return your neighbor's Tupperware, and another to sleep with her husband. For a small insensitivity, a simple and heartfelt "I'm sorry" may be all it takes, but not all of our insensitivities are simple.

This book will teach you how to craft a deeply meaningful apology, and decode apologies that are blame-reversing, ambiguous, and downright mean. Going beyond the "how-to's" of the good apology, we'll be looking at compelling stories that illustrate how much the simple apology matters and why we so often muck it up. We'll also be looking at heroic apologies that can open the door to forgiveness and healing in even the most difficult circumstances.

As the title *Why Won't You Apologize?* suggests, the chapters ahead are also for the hurt or angry person who has received a weaselly or insincere apology—or none at all. When we've been insulted or injured by someone who just doesn't get it, we can learn the steps necessary to change the tone of the conversation and get through. Other times, however, nothing we say or do will change the unrepentant wrongdoer. In fact, the more serious the harm, the less likely it is for the wrongdoer to feel genuine remorse and make amends. What does the hurt party do then?

The challenge of apology and reconciliation is a dance that occurs between at least two people. We are all, many times over, on both sides of the equation. Let's begin with a brief "sorry sampler"—*sorrys* that go from easy to medium to hard.

THE SIMPLEST "I'M SORRY"

The simplest "I'm sorry," the one easiest to offer, is when nothing is anybody's fault. We say these two words not as an apology but rather as an empathic response to another person's pain ("I'm so sorry you have to go through this ordeal"), or to a situation that has inconvenienced them ("I'm sorry I'm late. An accident on the interstate tied up the traffic"). Here, "I'm sorry" recognizes that the other person was put out or going through a difficult time, and we want to communicate that we care.

In many situations, saying "I'm sorry" requires relatively little effort—but the failure to extend it is not a small omission. Life is hard, and even the briefest of interactions with strangers can brighten your day or haunt it. It's not that you're going to sink into a major depression because the woman in the supermarket nearly ran you down with her trolley, and rushed off without even looking up. You might assume that she failed to apologize because she didn't care, or, alternatively, that she was too preoccupied or overcome with shame to make eye contact and speak. Whatever her reasons, it just doesn't feel good, and the not-good feeling hangs on. Sometimes, the failure of the other person to apologize when they should hits us harder than the deed they should apologize for.

The Long Wait in the Examining Room

When the relationship matters, the failure to say "I'm sorry" can erode connection, even when it's clear to both parties that no one is responsible for behaving badly. Consider my therapy client Yolanda, who sat clothed in a skimpy hospital gown on a cold table in the examining room waiting for her doctor, who was nearly an hour late.

"So, my doctor finally appears," Yolanda tells me, obviously upset, "and she says *nothing*, not even a simple apology. I felt like I wasn't even a person to her. And later I felt bad about myself for being so oversensitive."

Questioning ourselves for being "oversensitive" is a common way that women, in particular, disqualify our legitimate anger and hurt. If you've hung out in medical examining rooms, you know that patients feel vulnerable. The fact that some of us feel more vulnerable than others in a particular context does not mean we are weak or lesser in any way.

Yolanda didn't take the long wait personally. She didn't suspect that her physician was hiding out playing video games or texting her friends. Yolanda simply wanted to hear, "I'm sorry you had to wait so long. My last patient required more time than I had scheduled." The failure of Yolanda's doctor to even comment on her lateness felt like a small crack in a relationship with someone on whom she profoundly depends. A simple "I'm sorry" would have allowed Yolanda to feel respected, cared for, and validated.

A MEDIUM-DIFFICULT "I'M SORRY"

An apology is more difficult to offer when we *do* have something to apologize for and we regret our earlier behavior. Here even a short, sweet, and belated apology can sometimes matter a great deal.

Deborah, a therapy client of mine, missed her younger sister's wedding because it conflicted with a professional conference where she was presenting a paper. The conference had been scheduled long before her sister, Skye, decided on her wedding date, and Deborah was angry with her sister for expecting her to be there, and for insisting that the date she chose to marry was the only one that worked. But on the day of the wedding, Deborah felt awful about the choice she had made, and wished she were with her family at such an important time.

Though they moved on, the incident rankled both of them. At first, Deborah had no intention of apologizing to Skye. For one thing, she thought Skye should offer the apology. There was no excuse, Deborah told me, for announcing the wedding date as a "done deal" rather than factoring Deborah's schedule into the equation. Later, after feeling like she had made a colossal mistake in choosing to be at the conference, Deborah didn't want to reopen the issue for a different reason. Apologizing, she believed, would only amplify the issue and make them both feel worse.

Years later, in a flash of sudden affection for her sister, Deborah spontaneously sent Skye an email that said: "I've never told you how bad I felt about missing your wedding and how sorry I am about my decision. The day I was giving my paper at that conference, I kept thinking to myself, WHAT AM I DOING HERE? I have no explanation or excuse for making such a stupid decision." Her sister wrote back, "Yeah, Deb, you were a real asshole. :-)"

Email is generally not a good way to offer an apology. In this case, however, Deborah told me how everything felt lighter between them after this exchange. "It's like some bit of trust or closeness has been restored that I didn't even know was missing."

JUMPING OFF THE HIGH DIVE—
THE TOUGHEST APOLOGIES

It can take great courage to open a conversation and apologize for something we wish we had handled differently in the past. Perhaps we don't want to be intrusive, or we're concerned about how our apology will be received and what would happen next. If the other person hasn't brought the subject up we may assume that we shouldn't, either. But, as Margaret's story illustrates, it's best to leave open the possibility of talking about our earlier behavior that we now regret.

Margaret has a daughter, Eleanor, a single mother whose second child, Christian, died when he was sixteen days old, having never left the hospital. Margaret had been helpful in practical ways, taking care of Eleanor's three-year-old son, and keeping up the household during the two weeks Eleanor practically lived in the hospital.

Margaret was absent, however, at the emotional level. In true British fashion, she had a "no mess, no fuss" attitude toward life's difficulties, and a long cultural tradition of "Don't fret, plod on." She loved her daughter enormously, but she didn't want Eleanor to get bogged down in grief. She also wanted to avoid her own deep sorrow. Out of her wish to protect both Eleanor and herself, Margaret failed to express her pain or inquire how her daughter was doing with this profound loss. The few times she saw Eleanor crying or depressed, she said things like, "Your son needs you. Be strong for him."

A decade later, Margaret's coworker and friend, Jorge, had a son who was born stillborn. His loss understandably brought up Margaret's own buried feelings of grief about her grandson Christian and the life he never had. When she observed the tremendous outpouring of love that Jorge received, and the openhearted way that he embraced the caring that surrounded him, something shifted in Margaret. She asked herself for the first time if she had done right by her daughter in the way she had responded to Christian's tragic death.

Soon thereafter a newspaper article about untimely loss appeared on the front page of their local paper. Much to her own surprise, Margaret worked up her courage and asked Eleanor if she'd read the piece. She also told her that she thought about Christian all the time. Margaret went on to say that she regretted never talking about her feelings because she didn't know what to say and was afraid of making Eleanor feel worse. She said she was sorry that she had not made a space for them to talk about something so important, the saddest thing that had ever happened in their lives.

Eleanor's initial response was predictable. "There's nothing you could have done," she said flatly. "It wasn't something you could fix. Don't worry about it." Eleanor was very much her mother's daughter.

Often the most interesting part of an apology is what happens later. Neither brought the subject up again, but Margaret told me that after the initial awkwardness passed she felt better about having spoken up. Months later, as the anniversary of Christian's death was approaching, Margaret felt the desire to bring flowers to Christian's grave. She hadn't been there since the funeral. She casually mentioned this to Eleanor, who matter-of-factly replied that she planned to make the trip, and they could go together if Margaret wanted a lift.

Only on the way to the cemetery did Margaret learn that Eleanor had been to the graveside twice a year for the past ten years. As they stood by Christian's small gravestone, Margaret suddenly started sobbing. This surge of emotion took her totally by surprise because she had never cried about Christian's death, and hardly ever about anything else. More unexpected still, Eleanor put her arms around her mother and they cried together.

In Margaret's case her apology felt like a great risk. She had been raised in a family where cheerfulness was one of the few permissible emotions, and competence and independence (defined as not needing anybody) were next to godliness. Her apology required her to share vulnerability and take a big leap into the unknown. She had no role model from her past to look to as a guide, so pioneering a new path required great courage on her part.

BEYOND THE "HOW-TO'S"

There are, of course, far more difficult situations in which to apologize than Margaret's. For example, we may be faced with a person who wants us to apologize and we don't think we should. It's a profound challenge to sit on the hot seat and listen with an open heart to the hurt and anger of the wounded person who wants us to be sorry, especially when that person is accusing us (and not accurately, as we see it) of causing their pain. Yet both personal integrity and success in relationships depend on our ability to take responsibility for our part (and only our part) even when the other person is being a jerk.

In the following chapters, we'll take a fresh look at the power and potential pitfalls of apologies. For example:

* *Why is it so difficult for humans to offer clear expressions of responsibility and remorse for our hurtful words and actions?*

* *What drives the non-apologizer—and the female over-apologizer?*

* *Why are the people who do the worst things the least able to own up?*

* *How do we sort out who is responsible for what?*

* *How do we (the hurt party) unwittingly contribute to the other person's defensiveness and refusal to apologize?*

* *How can we get past life-draining anger and bitterness when the wrongdoer distorts reality or reverses blame?*

* *What's the real reason you can't stop hating your ex (or whoever)?*

Perhaps the most painful issue in the apology lexicon is coming to terms with the nonrepentant wrongdoer. This is a universal human challenge for which forgiveness is the prescribed solution of the day. Yet as we'll see, you do not need to forgive the person who has hurt you in order to free yourself from obsessive anger and bitterness. Indeed, sometimes you have to be brave enough to resist pressure from the forgiveness police.

The need for apologies and repair is a singularly human one—both on the giving and receiving ends. We are hardwired to seek justice and fairness (however we see it), so the need to receive a sincere apology that's due is deeply felt. We are also imperfect human beings and prone to error and defensiveness, so the challenge of offering a heartfelt apology permeates almost every relationship.

We take turns at being the offender and the offended until our very last breath. It's reassuring to know that we have the possibility to set things right, or at least to know that we have brought our best selves to the task at hand, however the other person responds.

CHAPTER 2

Five Ways to Ruin
an Apology

Many well-intentioned people want to apologize and genuinely don't know how. They've said "I'm sorry" and don't understand why the hurt party doesn't soften up. Recognizing the most common ingredients of a failed apology will lay the groundwork for knowing how to offer a successful one.

An effective apology involves more than saying the right words and avoiding the wrong ones, but it helps to know the difference. Let's start with "A Beginner's Guide to Bad Apologies"—five ways "I'm sorry" can go south. Later we'll look at the challenge of heroic apologies that can open the door to forgiveness and healing in even the most difficult circumstances.

RAISING OUR "BUT" CONSCIOUSNESS

More than anything, the hurt party wants to hear an apology that is heartfelt. When "but" is tagged on to an apology, it undoes the sincerity. Watch out for this sneaky little add-on. It almost always signals an excuse or cancels out the original message. It doesn't matter if the statement you make after the "but" is true—it makes the apology false. It says, in effect, "Given the whole situation, my rudeness (or lateness, or sarcastic tone, or what-have-you) is pretty understandable."

Consider my friend Dolores, who was irritated that her younger sister didn't lift a finger at their family reunion when everyone else was pitching in. At one point, Dolores felt a rush of anger, and criticized her sister in front of other family members. "You're not the guest of honor at this party," Dolores barked. "Would it really kill you to load the dishwasher?" No surprise that her feedback didn't go down well. Her sister walked away and they avoided each other for the remainder of the gathering.

Dolores felt badly. A few days after returning home, she called her sister to apologize for being out of line. "I apologize for the way I confronted you, but I have a very hard time with you not pulling your weight. It reminds me how I did all the chores growing up and Mom always let you get away with doing nothing because she hated fighting with you. I apologize for being rude, but someone had to tell you how to act."

"That's not an apology," I noted, when Dolores complained that her sister didn't respond positively. Understandably, it was incredibly difficult for Dolores to offer a genuine apology for her rudeness when she carried so much anger and resentment from the past. But I imagine her sister might have felt insulted all over again. Embedded in Delores's "apology" was the implication that not only had her sister acted like a spoiled brat at the reunion, but she had occupied this role her entire life. And "someone had to tell you how to act" is an obvious dig.

Perhaps Dolores's sister would have been more open to accepting the apology if Dolores had simply said she was terribly sorry for being rude and out of line. Rather than ramping up her sister's level of defensiveness, a simple apology might have provided her sister with the space to consider her own behavior at the reunion.

Dolores's intentions were good. "I wanted to give my sister some background as to why I overreacted," she told me. "I wanted her to know that my reaction to her not pulling her weight has a long history."

Fine, but that's a different conversation, and one that Dolores might open with a good measure of timing and tact. The best apologies are short, and don't go on to include explanations that run the risk of undoing them. An apology isn't the only chance you ever get to address the underlying issue. The apology is the chance you get to establish the ground for future communication. This is an important and often overlooked distinction.

"I'M SORRY YOU FEEL THAT WAY"

"I'm sorry you feel that way" is another common pseudo-apology. A true apology keeps the focus on your actions—and not on the other person's response.

Consider my recent crazy-making experience with a guy I'll call Leon. Leon was in charge of promotion for an organization that had invited me to give a lecture. The organization had an old photo of me taken about twenty years ago, so I sent Leon a new one that was up to date. "Please use this one," I said. When I showed up at the event, I wanted to resemble myself.

Maybe it was a careless mistake, or maybe Leon thought a younger-looking presenter would draw a bigger audience, but he posted the wrong photo online, and then again (even after I pointed out his mistake) in the printed material. Our final conversation went like this:

> ME: *What happened? You posted the photo from two decades ago online. After we talked about this mistake, you used the same photo in the brochure.*

> LEON: *I used the photo that came up in my computer. I can't pay attention to every detail. I'm not perfect.*

> ME: *This isn't about perfection. I just want to use a recent photo.*

> LEON: *I'm sorry that the photo is so important to you. I don't think that the participants are as involved as you are in how you look.*

> ME: *The point is that I asked you to use the photo I supplied.*

* Five Ways to Ruin an Apology *

LEON: *Okay, I apologize, I'm sorry that you're feeling so upset about your photo. I didn't know this was such a sensitive issue for you.*

Leon was not a genuine apologizer. He tried to make *me* the problem, implying my pickiness or vanity was at fault, not his failure to abide by our agreement. If he were my therapy client, I would simply have brought my objective and curious eye to the interesting way he muddled reality to avoid taking responsibility for a simple error. Since I'm not his therapist, Leon's combination of disrespect, incompetence, and defensiveness infuriated me. I would have much preferred that Leon not apologize at all, since he evidently didn't care, wasn't sorry, never corrected the online error, and blamed me for making a big deal out of what he considered to be nothing. Or perhaps he knew full well he'd done wrong but didn't want to take responsibility for it. Whatever Leon's experience, a false, blame-reversing apology is worse than no apology because it repeats and deepens the insensitivity.

You may not identify one bit with Leon, but one of the common ways that we can slither away from taking responsibility is by apologizing for the other person's feelings, rather than for specific behavior on our part. "I'm sorry you felt embarrassed when I corrected your story at the party" is not an apology. There is no accountability here. You may get to feel good about yourself for taking the moral high ground (you've apologized), while really you've shifted the responsibility to the other person. You're saying, in effect, "I'm sorry that you overreacted to my perfectly reasonable comments." Instead try, "I'm sorry I corrected your story at the party. I get it. And I won't do it again."

Watch Out for "IF"

The little word *if* also invites the other person to question their own reactions. Watch out for, "I'm sorry if I was insensitive," or "I'm sorry if you took what I said as offensive." Almost any apology that begins with "I'm sorry if . . ." is a non-apology. Try instead, "The comment I made was offensive. I'm sorry I was insensitive and I want you to know that it won't happen again."

"I'm sorry if" can also come across as condescending. At a team meeting, a therapy client of mine, Charles, made a tasteless joke about the "female brain." Afterward, he said to his boss, "I'm sorry if my comment hurt your feelings." Her snappy response was, "Believe me, Charles, my feelings are not so easily hurt." The anger in her voice puzzled him. He didn't understand that he was suggesting that his superior was an overly sensitive woman, rather than apologizing for making a comment that was out of line.

I don't want to sound like the language police here, but I encourage you to pay attention to the teensy add-on words that will turn your "I'm sorry" into a "not really sorry at all."

THE MYSTIFYING APOLOGY

A father I saw in therapy with his teenage son had a short fuse and often reacted with harsh criticism when his son made small mistakes, such as not closing a tricky garage door properly. When he saw how upset his son became, he would apologize by saying, "I'm sorry that what I said to you made you so upset." It was his standard apology for all things.

"I hate his apology," his son told me. "It bothers me and I don't know why." The son knew something didn't feel right, but he wasn't able to identify the mystifying nature of an apology that obfuscated what the dad was apologizing for, and who had the problem. He just knew that his dad's apology left him feeling uncomfortable and off balance.

This dad's non-apology didn't reflect defensiveness or a sneaky attempt to avoid responsibility. It rather reflected the confused thinking that typifies anxious families. The higher the anxiety in any system, the more individuals are held responsible for *other* people's feelings and behavior ("Apologize to your dad for giving him a headache") rather than for their own ("Apologize to your dad for not turning the music down when you knew he had a headache").

"Look What You're Making Him Do!"

Here is a mystifying apology that I will never forget— never mind that it happened decades ago. When my older son Matt was about six years old, he was playing with a classmate, Sean. At some point Matt grabbed the boy's toy out of his hand and refused to give it back. The boy began knocking his head against the wooden floor and didn't stop.

The boy's mother was close by, and she reacted quickly and with considerable intensity. She did not tell her son to stop banging his head, nor did she tell Matt to return her son's toy. Instead, she turned to Matt with this stern reprimand: "Do you see what you are doing, Matt?" she said, pointing to her head-banging child. "Look at what you are doing! You are making Sean bang his head on the floor. You apologize to him right now!"

Matt looked confused, and understandably so. He was not being asked to apologize for grabbing Sean's toy. He was being asked to apologize for Sean banging his head. Rather than Matt being held accountable for his own behavior, he was asked to take responsibility for the other boy's reactions. Matt handed the toy back and walked away, no apology offered. Later I mentioned to Matt that he should have apologized for taking Sean's toy, but that he wasn't to blame for Sean banging his head.

If Matt had taken responsibility for Sean's head-banging, Matt's apology would have been at his own expense. He would have been admitting to something he did not—and could not—do. It would equally have been at Sean's expense, who then would be denied the agency and responsibility to manage his anger in a different way.

"FORGIVE ME—AND DO IT NOW!"

Another fine way to ruin an apology is to view your apology as an automatic ticket to forgiveness and redemption, that is, it's really about you and your need for reassurance. "I'm sorry" shouldn't be viewed as a bargaining chip you give to get something back from the injured party, like forgiveness.

The words "Do you forgive me?" or "Please forgive me" are a valued ritual in certain close relationships, and it's fine to apologize and ask for forgiveness if you are in a relationship where the hurt party appreciates this. But if you as the wrongdoer expect or demand forgiveness, or request it prematurely, you may end up with a failed apology. Here's an example.

Don let his fourteen-year-old daughter take a motorcycle ride with a biker friend. His wife, Sylvia, didn't want her daughter on a motorcycle with anyone, and Don had long ago promised to honor this request. When he broke his promise, he asked his daughter to keep the ride a secret from her mother, "because we both know she would freak out."

When their daughter spilled the beans a few days later, Sylvia was enraged. Don was appropriately penitent for his inappropriate behavior—the motorcycle ride and the secret-keeping pact he'd made with his daughter. He apologized up and down and swore he'd never do it again. Then he pressured Sylvia to forgive him.

When Sylvia said, "I don't forgive you!" Don kept

the pressure on. What he might have said was: "I understand that what I did was serious and you may stay angry for a long time. If there is anything I can do to make it better, please let me know."

Sylvia felt crowded by Don's insistence that she forgive him, which gave her less emotional space to arrive at a place of genuine forgiveness that came from within her and not from feeling backed into a corner. The situation worsened when Don became angry at her failure to forgive. Now Sylvia felt like Don had turned the tables by putting himself in the victim role. She had no room to forgive him at all.

Keep in mind that offering an apology, followed too quickly by a request for forgiveness, can cut short the necessary emotional process of the hurt party. The hurt party, put on the spot, and feeling grateful or relieved to receive the apology, may too hastily "forgive" without allowing herself time to sit with her anger and pain.

When we offer a genuine apology, it's only natural to want our apology to lead to forgiveness and reconciliation, but demanding forgiveness can undercut an apology by making the other person feel rushed and even wronged all over again. Apologies often need their own time and space to take hold.

THE INTRUSIVE APOLOGY

There is nothing good to be said about apologizing to someone who truly does not want to hear another word from you.

A woman named Liza slept with the husband of her friend Celina. Celina was clear with Liza that she wanted no further contact with her. Celina put Liza out of her mind, as best as she could, as she and her husband worked to heal their marriage after the affair was out in the open.

Several years later, when Liza was working the twelve steps in her AA program, her sponsor encouraged her to examine her actions to see if she had harmed anyone in her past, and advised her to pick up her phone and make direct amends. Liza got Celina's cell phone number from a mutual acquaintance and left a voice message saying that sleeping with Celina's husband was the worst mistake she had ever made, and that she wanted to meet for coffee so she could make amends and tell her part of the story.

Celina felt re-traumatized hearing Liza's voice on the phone, and Liza's request stirred up all the tumultuous feelings that she had worked so hard to put aside. Liza called a second time with the same message, adding, "I think that if you know my part of the story, you might be able to forgive me." When Celina wisely chose not to respond, Liza then sent her a letter probably expressing more of the same, and Celina tossed it unopened into the recycling bin. Liza's insistence on reentering Celina's life felt to Celina like another violation.

Liza does need to forgive herself, but her process of self-forgiveness should not involve contacting Celina. The purpose of an apology is to calm and soothe the hurt party, not to agitate or pursue her because you have the impulse to connect, explain yourself, lower your guilt quotient, or foster your recovery. The AA step Liza followed encourages making amends only when doing so will not injure the hurt party or others. Not everyone, however, can make that distinction.

CHAPTER 3

More Wimpy, Overblown, and Downright Relationship-Busting Sorrys

"I wish you could hear a voice recording of my former colleague," my niece tells me. "She constantly apologizes for random things that obviously need no apology. It forces the person at the other end of the conversation to constantly say things like, 'No, not at all, it's fine,' instead of whatever you wanted to talk about."

If some people can't get the words "I'm sorry" out of their mouth, others, largely female, apologize to a fault. Women in my generation were raised to feel guilty if we were anything less than an emotional service station to others. We may be quick to feel responsible for everything. As comedian and writer Amy Poehler puts it, "It takes years as a woman to unlearn what you have been taught to be sorry for."

I have a friend in California who apologizes so

much I want to kick her under the table. The last time we gathered at a restaurant with several other friends, she offered five apologies (yes, I counted) before our waiter brought out appetizers.

"Oh, I'm sorry, did you want to sit by the window?" "Oh, I interrupted you. I'm sorry, please go ahead." "Oh, is this your menu? I'm so sorry." "Oh, I'm sorry, were you just about to order?" When we walk on narrow sidewalks, we frequently bump hips, and again it's "Oh, sorry," even though I most likely bumped into her, being the infinitely more clumsy one. If I knocked her off the sidewalk, I'm quite certain she would look up from her prone position and say, "Oh, I'm so sorry."

Maybe I get irritated because I'm a cranky New Yorker and she's from the South, where she was taught to leave food on her plate at every meal for "Miss Manners." Each of her apologies is said so politely and deliberately that you'd think she went to the Miss Manners Apology Finishing School, an observation I couldn't resist telling her, since our friendship dates back to college, and she knows I love her. Some people are impressed with her grace and good manners, but the *sorrys* are too much.

Even women with impeccable feminist credentials are prone to this problem. As feminist scholar Maggie Nelson writes, "Over the years I've had to train myself to wipe the sorry off almost every work e-mail I write; otherwise, each might begin, *Sorry for the delay, Sorry for the confusion, Sorry for whatever.*"

Watch out for meaningless over-apologizing. Save your apologies for things that matter.

What's Over-Apologizing About?

What drives over-apologizing? We can never know for sure. It may be a reflection of low self-esteem, a diminished sense of entitlement, an unconscious wish to avoid any possibility of criticism or disapproval before it even occurs, an excessive wish to placate and please, some underlying river of shame, or a desire to show off what a well-mannered Brownie Scout one is. Or, alternatively, the reflexive "I'm sorrys" may be nothing more than a verbal tick, a little self-effacing girl-thing that developed long ago, and now is something like an automatic hiccough.

You don't need to know what causes something in order to fix it. If you over-apologize, tone it down. If you've forgotten to return your friend's salad bowl, don't apologize numerous times, as if you ran over her kitten. Over-apologizing creates distance and interrupts the normal flow of conversation. It will irritate your friends, and also make it harder for them to hear you when you offer an apology that you really need to give.

DON'T CRY SOMEONE ELSE'S TEARS

Part of a true apology involves showing empathy and remorse. Without authentic feeling behind your apology, it may sound robotic and insincere. Yet, it's also possible to overdo the *mea culpa*. It's not a true apology if overdoing how terrible you feel about your misdeed leaves the hurt party feeling worse. This story from my therapy practice may illustrate the point.

In a moment of distracted driving, Amy ran a stop sign and hit another car, with her sixteen-year-old daughter, Rebecca, in the passenger seat next to her. Amy escaped with minor bruises, but Rebecca sustained serious injuries that required two surgeries and an extended period of physical therapy and rehabilitation.

Amy was an excellent driver. It was her first accident, and one that might have happened to any of us. Of course, she was beside herself with guilt, grief, and remorse. The fact that her daughter never pointed a finger at her or uttered a critical word only increased Amy's dread of her daughter's unspoken anger. Several times a day, if not more, Amy would tell her daughter how sorry she was, and how she would never forgive herself. When Rebecca expressed emotional distress or physical pain, Amy would sometimes cry, and Rebecca would comfort her. Over and over Amy said, "If only it was me, not you. I would do anything to change places with you!"

Rebecca began to feel angry, crowded, and disempowered by her mother's focus on how painful it was to see her suffer. "Enough already!" she shouted at Amy one morning. "This is *my* suffering, and I'll deal with it. Go take *your* suffering someplace else." Amy, to her credit, got the message. She entered therapy with me to cope with her guilt and grief, and she toned down her emotionality with Rebecca.

Amy's expressions of guilt and remorse were deeply felt, and Rebecca needed to see her mother's authentic sorrow. It would not have been helpful to offer an apology that failed to show Rebecca that her mother was carrying some of the pain. It was simply a matter of degree. *Overdoing* the expression of these feelings, and failing to tone down the intensity, placed a burden on Rebecca, who felt she had to take care of her mother's pain, rather than give voice to her own and put her full energy into her own healing.

A Good Apology Is Not About You

Part of a true apology is staying deeply curious about the hurt person's experience rather than hijacking it with your own emotionality. As Amy's story illustrates, a problem occurs when the conversation ends up with the hurt or angry party focusing on *your* pain. When this happens, you've lost the opportunity to offer a genuine apology and the other person may leave the conversation feeling awful.

Mary, a thirty-four-year-old social worker who attended an anger workshop I gave in Minneapolis, told me this: *"I can't talk to my mother about anything she might take as a criticism. The same thing always happens. Her apologies are so full of remorse and self-recrimination that I end up reassuring her that she was a good mother and she did the best she could. Later I feel like crap."*

It won't help to say you're sorry and then act forlorn and beleaguered as if the other person had just rubbed your face in a plate of dog food. Nor does it help to say you're sorry and somehow convey that the person you really feel sorry for is yourself, and the hurt party needs to understand how wrenching your own situation is or was, or how deeply ashamed and worthless you feel now that you realize that you're such a big failure, and maybe you should never open your mouth again since you always seem to say the wrong thing.

Being *too* sorry can be a covert form of defensiveness. If the hurt party starts feeling the need to make you, the offending party, feel better, take it as a signal to tone down the emotionality and dial back your defensiveness. A heartfelt apology is not about you. If your intention is to offer a genuine apology, it's the hurt party's anger and pain that matters. Save yours for a different conversation.

DON'T *UNDERDO!*

Underdoing an apology can be equally offensive. While visiting a friend in Chicago I was trapped in a hotel lift for forty-five minutes, which felt like forty-five years. It was after midnight, the alarm button appeared not to work, and it was a terrifying experience.

I learned that this wasn't the first time the elevator had malfunctioned and not been adequately fixed. I called the appropriate person and also wrote her a letter of complaint. Her response was, "I'm very sorry for the inconvenience this caused you. We will take care of the problem as soon as possible."

"*Inconvenience!* Maybe *you* should experience the *inconvenience* of being trapped alone in an elevator in the middle of the night!" was what I wanted to say but didn't. Her choice of words didn't sit well with me. And when underdoing occurs in a relationship that matters, the hurt caused by a wimpy apology is obviously deeper and more lasting.

"I'm sorry" may also feel empty and halfhearted if there's no attempt to make restitution. Friends of mine, a couple who live on a tight budget, recently splurged on a big celebration for their first anniversary. They went to a fancy restaurant in Kansas City, where the service at their table was unspeakably bad. I imagine the kitchen was understaffed that night, because it took forever for them to get their appetizers, and even longer than forever to get the main course and the cheque. They had mentioned up front that they had concert tickets and needed to be out of there at a particular time, so the waitstaff knew their situation.

The wife complained to their waiter and asked him to take their complaints to the manager, who appeared on the spot. He said he was terribly sorry that the service had been so slow, and told them he would talk to the people in the kitchen about the problem. He said "I'm terribly sorry" at least three times.

What he did *not* say was, "The wine is on us," or "The appetizers are on the house." He showed no interest in making some gesture that would have set things right. He may have saved himself some money, but he ensured that they would never return, or recommend the restaurant to their friends.

The failure to make restitution is bad business in our personal relationships as well. If, for example, you apologize ten times for spilling coffee on your friend's rug, but you don't get up from the couch to help clean up, nor offer to pay for the cleaning bill should there be one, it's not a real apology. Similarly, if you're apologizing for having planned an out-of-town trip on your best friend's birthday, it will help if you immediately take the initiative to make an alternative plan that reflects thoughtfulness and care.

THE GOOD ENOUGH APOLOGY

Failed apologies don't just occur in our personal transactions. Apologies abound in the public and political sphere as well, where remorse is fake, accountability is absent, and blame is shifted to the wrongdoer. Much has been written about the slippery and sneaky language used by public figures, such as politicians ("Mistakes were made . . ."), celebrities, and business and community leaders. But none of us is immune from delivering self-serving faux-apologies, often without even intending to.

The formula for a good enough apology seems pretty straightforward. In his book *Effective Apology*, business expert John Kador's definition is as good as any I've seen: "We apologize when we accept responsibility for an offence or grievance and express remorse in a direct, personal and unambiguous manner, offering restitution and promising not to do it again." A good apology includes the words "I'm sorry" without "ifs," "buts," or any manner of undoings, obfuscations, and the like. Yet we've seen how easy it is to slip into language that distances us from responsibility and that muddles exactly what we are apologizing for.

Furthermore, no one formula fits all. As Gary Chapman and Jennifer Thomas point out in *The Five Languages of Apology*, the "right way" to say you're sorry depends on whom you are apologizing to, because people differ in the words they need to hear in order to accept an apology as sincere. Words that soothe one person may disappoint or irritate another. One person may need to hear the offender say, "I was wrong," in order to feel that the apology is genuine. For another person, "I promise to do my best to ensure it won't happen again" are the magic words that allow the apology to get through.

Then there's the matter of what you're apologizing for. To heal a large hurt, a simple and genuine "I'm sorry" is only a good *first* step. More needs to follow in order to set things right. As the next chapter illustrates, high-stakes situations call for an apology that's a long-distance run—one that may require us to sit on the hot seat and listen with an open heart to the anger of the wounded party on more than one occasion. There is no greater gift, or one more difficult to offer, than the gift of wholehearted listening to that sort of pain.

CHAPTER 4

Apologizing Under Fire: How to Handle Big-Time Criticism

I t's difficult enough to offer an apology when we see the need for it and believe it's the right thing to do. It's far more difficult still when we're confronted with criticism we didn't see coming, and that we don't believe is fair. Some criticism we receive will undoubtedly come from the other person's reactivity rather than our bad behavior.

No one likes being on the receiving end of criticism, but we can't avoid it unless we sit mute in a corner. People are bound to criticize us for the same reasons we criticize them. They may feel badly about themselves, and reflexively get judgmental or lash out. They may have a misguided wish to be helpful and contribute to our betterment. Or we have a trait, quality, or behavior that bothers them enough that they really do need to talk about it or it will affect the relationship. They may feel, quite accurately, that the relationship can't move forward if we don't consider our behavior and apologize for it.

It is incredibly difficult to sit on the hot seat and tone down our defensiveness when we are the target of criticism that feels overdone or entirely undeserved. But as the story of Katherine and Dee will illustrate, a lot can be learned from the challenge. We can learn to listen differently, to ask questions, to apologize for the part we can agree with and define how we see things differently. A genuine apology can be deeply healing, while the failure to listen well and apologize can sometimes lead to the loss of a relationship.

UNEARTHING OLD PAIN: KATHERINE AND DEE

It was Christmas Eve. Dee, who was twenty-six years old, had driven four hours to spend time with her mother, Katherine, who had divorced Dee's dad when Dee was nine. They were cleaning up after the small party Katherine had thrown when out of the blue Dee turned to her mother and said those dreaded four words, "We have to talk."

Dee's timing wasn't great and her list of grievances was devastating. She accused Katherine of neglecting her around the time of the divorce and noted that her own suffering had gone entirely unattended because, in Dee's words, "You were too narcissistic to get over yourself and take care of me." She held her mother responsible for her (Dee's) problems with men and for her bleak prospects for future relationships. She also blamed her mother for her father's drinking after the divorce. Dee mentioned that she had uncovered these insights in therapy, which Katherine happened to be paying for.

Katherine came to see me in therapy two months later. When she told me this story she was shaking with rage, and said that at the time of Dee's confrontation, it took everything she had not to attack back. Trying to hold it together, Katherine had offered the closest thing to an apology that she could muster. She said, "I'm sorry, Dee, that you had such a hard time with the divorce. I never meant to hurt you. I did the best I could. So whatever I did wrong, I'm sorry." Then she said good night and went to bed.

Decoding a Faux-Apology

Given that Katherine was blindsided by the attack, it's no surprise that she offered a classic non-apology. In case you didn't recognize it as such, here's a translation:

> "I'm sorry, Dee, that you had such a hard time with the divorce."
> *(Your reaction to the divorce is the unfortunate problem here.)*

> "I never meant to hurt you."
> *(I'm a good person and I didn't do anything wrong.)*

"I did the best I could."
(And what more can you say to that!)

"So whatever I did wrong, I'm sorry."
(If I did something wrong, I'm clueless about what it is.
But I'm sorry, so let's move on.)

This analysis is by no means a criticism of how Katherine handled herself. It's remarkable she didn't strike back. Who among us would have done better under the circumstances?

Who's Going to Apologize First?

Katherine told me that there had been zero communication between her and Dee since this devastating confrontation, and she had no plans to initiate contact. "I said I was sorry," Katherine told me, "and now I'm waiting for Dee to apologize for her outrageous attack."

But if Katherine was waiting for her daughter to apologize first, I suspected that she would be waiting a very long time. Katherine's pseudo-apology ("I'm sorry you had such a hard time with the divorce") and clichéd excuse ("I did the best I could") certainly wouldn't be satisfying to her daughter. Dee hadn't apologized yet and might never do so.

I asked Katherine what she wanted her relationship with Dee to look like by next Christmas or, say, five years in the future. For how long could Katherine tolerate having no contact with her daughter—weeks, months, years? However she chose to respond to her daughter, whether through words or silence, would either de-escalate the situation or intensify it. If Katherine had stayed focused on getting her daughter to apologize first, nothing might have changed at all.

It didn't take too long in therapy before Katherine told me that she was afraid of losing her daughter. As she explored her options, she realized she was still too angry to pick up the phone, and she certainly didn't feel like apologizing for her "bad mothering." Nor did I encourage her to apologize, because any apology Katherine offered from a position of anger and distance would have been false and entirely without meaning. As Katherine's therapist I wanted to help her to calm down and think about the bigger picture.

Breaking a Multigenerational Pattern

As Katherine talked in therapy about family interactions across generations, it was clear that mothers and daughters had not fared especially well. The pattern was one of fighting on the one hand, or distance and cutoff on the other. Did Katherine want to follow this tradition with Dee? Obviously both mother and daughter had a lot at stake.

Dee's behavior was way out of line, perhaps the result of so many years of never giving voice to her anger and pain. But here is the real point when it comes to the challenge of apologies in family relationships. If our intention is to have a better relationship, we need to be our best and most mature self, rather than reacting to the other person's reactivity. Also, some of the other person's complaints will be true, since we can't possibly get it right all of the time.

Only after we can hear our children's criticism and anger, and are open to apologizing for the inevitable hurts and mistakes that every parent makes, can we expect to be truly heard by them. We need to be able to listen before we get our own message across—good advice for any relationship.

Laying the Groundwork: A Perfect Letter

What next? Katherine was an attorney with a fine eye for detail and impressive verbal skills, so her impulse was to write a long letter building her case—a step in the wrong direction if her goal was to have a better relationship with Dee, or to have any relationship at all.

At my suggestion, she instead put a short, warm message in a greeting card, noting that she knew the visit was difficult for both of them, and that she was trying to consider the things Dee had told her as openly as possible. Dee didn't respond to this card, or, more accurately, she responded with silence, which I encouraged Katherine not to take personally but rather view as information about Dee's level of reactivity.

A few weeks later, at my suggestion, Katherine sent Dee a handwritten note (not email) that went something like this:

Dear Dee,

I'm sitting here on the red couch wondering how you're doing. I've continued to think about your last visit. I'm sorry things got so intense between us. I assume from your silence that you need more space at this time.

I appreciate the courage it took for you to share your feelings so directly with me. I want to have the kind of relationship in which we can talk openly, something I never had with my own mother. I was never able to tell her when I was angry with her and I never stood up to her. Maybe that's why I felt so unprepared to handle conflict between you and me.

My mother told me that she and her mother were always fighting and they stopped speaking to each other for years. So she and I reacted to that bit of history by doing the opposite and never letting a difference arise between us, which made for a pretty superficial relationship.

As I think about how things went between mothers and daughters, I realize how much I hope that you and I can have a different kind of relationship. I've also been thinking about the people in our family who aren't speaking to each other. I can't imagine anything more painful than that happening between you and me. So let's try again when you're ready, and I'll do my best to listen.

Love, Mom

The letter that Katherine wrote her daughter illustrates seven family systems principles for creating a calm emotional field that will allow two people to talk together or even stay in the same room:

* *Katherine focused only on herself.*

* *There was no implied criticism or blame.*

* *She didn't request or demand a particular response from Dee.*

* *She broadened the frame around the issue of mothers and daughters.*

* *She stood for connection without getting preachy.*

* *She didn't overload the circuits by going on too long.*

* *She didn't push for contact before Dee was ready.*

Katherine wisely did not include an apology in this letter, because it would have been premature. What her daughter wanted more than anything was what we all want in our most important relationships. She wanted her mother to really get her experience and care about her feelings. She wanted her mother to listen. Understandably, listening to more of Dee's criticism was the last thing Katherine wanted to do.

Sitting on the Hot Seat

This time Dee responded to Katherine's letter, albeit briefly, saying she was swamped with work and would get back in touch when she could. Dee's response was an important sign that she wasn't entrenched in a position of cutoff. Not long afterward they were back on speaking terms.

Then came the hardest part. It's incredibly difficult to listen to someone's pain when that someone is accusing us of causing it. We automatically listen for and react to what is unfair and incorrect. To listen with an open heart and ask questions to better help us understand the other person is a spiritual exercise, in the truest sense of the word.

Katherine rose to the challenge because the relationship was so important to her and because she knew that this was what Dee needed her to do. She decided in advance that she would try to listen differently—that *all* she would do was to listen as openly as possible and ask questions that would better allow her to understand her daughter's feelings.

So at a calm time, she took the initiative to revisit the conversation. She asked Dee more about the ways the divorce affected her, both at the time it was happening and now in the present. She said, "At Christmas you said I ignored you around the time of the divorce. Can you tell me what you remember about that?"

It took tremendous effort to sit on the hot seat and *only* listen. When Dee again accused her mother of "selfish neglect," Katherine could feel the defensiveness rise in her body—that immediate, "But, but, but . . ." response that makes us tense and on guard, unable to hear what the other person is saying. She automatically wanted to counter Dee's story with her own view of the facts.

Dee was clueless about what her mother had been up against during the breakup of her marriage. Katherine had been depressed and without support after the divorce and physically exhausted by her efforts to stay afloat financially. To Katherine's great credit, she didn't hijack her daughter's story with her own. Instead she slowed down her breathing and did what she could to calm herself so she could continue to listen, thus laying the groundwork for a sincere apology, and a more growth-fostering connection. She would have a chance to tell her story later.

Offering a Genuine Apology

As Katherine listened to Dee's experience, she was able to access some real empathy. She let Dee know, in a sincere way, how sorry she was that she hadn't been more available to her during that painful time. She said she wished she could go back in time and do a better job of being there. She thanked her daughter for her honesty and expressed gratitude that Dee had the courage to bring up her real feelings.

More important than the words "I'm sorry" was Katherine's dedication to keeping the lines of communication open over time. She let Dee know that their conversation wouldn't slip out of her brain the next day, or ever. Katherine said, "It's not easy to hear what you're telling me, but I want you to know that what you're telling me is very important to me and I'm going to keep thinking about it. I hope you'll let me know as more comes up for you over time. I'll try to do the same."

The words *"I want you to know that I'm going to keep thinking about what you've told me"* are an often neglected and truly important part of a healing apology.

"Here's Where We See Things Differently"

An authentic apology doesn't mean that we passively accept criticisms that we believe are wrong, unjust, and totally off the mark. Katherine could let some of Dee's angry remarks go—a sign of Katherine's maturity and good judgment. At the same time, she needed to speak to a couple of her daughter's accusations that continued to upset her.

One point of disagreement concerned Dee's accusation that her mother was responsible for Dee's problems with men, past, present, and future. Katherine agreed that she had made mistakes in the past that certainly may have contributed to Dee's difficulties, but she did not agree that she was responsible for the decisions Dee made as an adult. So when the time felt right, she warmly explained to her daughter that she didn't see herself as causing Dee's poor choices with men, nor did she share Dee's pessimism about her bleak romantic future. In a loving way Katherine said, "I have more confidence in you and more hope for your future relationships than you may feel right now."

Katherine also told Dee that she took no responsibility for her dad's drinking after the divorce. She said, "As you know, when people divorce, they usually have quite different perspectives on what happened. But whatever happened between your dad and me, I take responsibility only for my behavior, not for his. He was an adult and his drinking was his problem. I regret that he didn't get the help he needed but I am not to blame for this." A sincere apology means we are fully accountable for the part we are responsible for, and for only that.

Katherine said that she understood that these were points they saw differently, and she wanted to have the kind of relationship where they talk about the places where they disagreed. She expressed herself clearly, without trying to change Dee or convince her of "the truth."

What started as a crisis and could have led to years of bitter silence became an opportunity for both Dee and Katherine to learn more about themselves and each other. The following Christmas, Dee surprised Katherine by apologizing for how severely she had confronted her mother the year before. It was an apology that Katherine never requested and that she needed increasingly less over time, but that was nonetheless deeply appreciated.

A Word About Being Blasted

A commitment to listening doesn't mean that we stay mute while the other person is rude and out of bounds.

It's important to have limits especially about tolerating unkindness. For example, at the time of the original confrontation, Katherine might have said, "Dee, what you're telling me is really important. But it's Christmas Eve, I'm exhausted, and I can't have this conversation now. Let's talk tomorrow after breakfast when I can really pay attention." Or, "Dee I love you, but I'm feeling flooded, and I can't take in what you're telling me all at once. I need to give myself a time-out. Let's talk in the morning when we're both rested."

Being a good listener also means that we can tell the other person when we can't listen—that we know when to say, "Not now" or "Not in this way." When we tolerate rudeness in any relationship—if doing so becomes habitual rather than a rare event—we erode our own self-regard and diminish the other person by not reaching for their competence to do better. Plus, there is nothing compassionate about letting a person go on and on when the conversation is at our expense or we just can't listen anymore.

HOW TO DIAL DOWN YOUR DEFENSIVENESS

I was taught in graduate school that listening is a passive process, but this is not true. Listening is an intensely active process, and one that comes far less naturally than talking. There is no greater challenge than that of listening without defensiveness, especially when we don't want to hear what the other person is telling us.

It's impossible to overstate how difficult it is to shift out of defensive mode. When someone approaches us in an angry or critical way, our automatic set point is listening for what we *don't* agree with. It's so automatic that it takes motivation, courage, and goodwill to observe our defensiveness and practice stepping away from it.

Nondefensive listening is at the heart of offering a sincere apology. Here are twelve points to keep in mind when we're on the receiving end of criticism:

1. *Recognize your defensiveness.* We are wired to go immediately into defensive mode when criticized. Becoming aware of our defensiveness can give us a tiny, crucial bit of distance from it. We are listening defensively when we listen for what we *don't* agree with. Catch yourself when you are focusing on the inaccuracies, distortions, and exaggerations that inevitably will be there.

2. *Breathe.* Defensiveness starts in the body, making us tense and on guard, unable to take in new information. Do what you can to calm yourself. Take slow and deep breaths.

3. *Listen only to understand.* Listen only to discover what you can agree with. Do not interrupt, argue, refute, or correct facts, or bring up your own criticisms and complaints. If your points are legitimate, that's all the more reason to save

them for a different conversation, when they can be a focus of conversation and not a defense strategy.

4. *Ask questions about whatever you don't understand.* When the criticism is vague ("I feel you don't respect me"), ask for a concrete example ("Can you give me another example where you felt I was putting you down?"). This will add to your clarity and show the other party that you care about understanding her. Note: Asking for specifics is not the same thing as nitpicking—the key is to be curious, not to cross-examine. Don't act like a lawyer, even if you are one.

5. *Find something you can agree with.* You may only agree with 7 percent of what the other person is saying, and still find a point of commonality. ("I think you're right that I was totally hogging the conversation the other night.") If you can't find anything to agree with, thank the other person for their openness, and let them know that you'll be thinking about what they've told you.

6. *Apologize for your part.* It will indicate to the critical party that you're capable of taking responsibility, not just evading it. It will also help shift the exchange out of combat into collaboration. Save your thoughts about *their* part until later.

7. *Let the offended party know he or she has been heard and that you will continue to think about the conversation.* Even if nothing has been resolved, tell the other person that she's reached you. ("It's not easy to hear what you're telling me, but I want you to know that I'm going to give it a lot of thought"). Take time to genuinely consider her point of view.

8. *Thank the critical person for sharing his or her feelings.* Relationships require that we take such initiative, and express gratitude where the other person might expect mere defensiveness. ("I appreciate your telling me this. I know it couldn't have been easy.") In this way we signal our commitment to the relationship.

9. *Take the initiative to bring the conversation up again.* Show the other person that you are continuing to think about her point of view and that you are willing to revisit the issue. ("I've been thinking about our conversation last week and I'm really glad that we had that talk. I'm wondering if there's more you haven't told me.")

10. *Draw the line at insults.* There may be a time to sit through an initial blast, but not if rudeness has become a pattern in your relationship rather than an uncommon occurrence. Exit from rudeness while offering the possibility of another con-

versation. ("I want to hear what bothers you, but I need you to approach me with respect.")

11. *Don't listen when you can't listen well.* It's fine to tell the other person that you want to have the conversation and that you recognize its importance, but you can't have it right now. If you're closing the conversation, suggest a specific window of time to resume it. ("I can't absorb what you're saying now. Let's come back to it tomorrow when I'll be able to give you my full attention.")

12. *Define your differences.* You need to tell the critical person how you see things differently, rather than being an overly accommodating, peace-at-any-price type of person who apologizes to avoid conflict. Even if the other person isn't able to consider your point of view, you may need to hear the sound of your own voice saying what you really think. Timing is crucial, so consider saving your different point of view for a future conversation when you'll have the best chance of being heard.

Words of apology, no matter how sincere, will not heal a broken connection if we haven't listened well to the hurt party's anger and pain. As we've seen, a good listener does more than sit there and make empathic grunts. Wholehearted listening requires us to quiet our mind, open our heart, and ask questions to help us to better understand. It also requires that we stop ourselves from interrupting, making corrections, and saying things that leave the other person feeling unheard or cut short. It requires us to get past our defensiveness when the critical party is saying things that we don't agree with and don't want to hear, and instead let her voice and her pain affect and influence us.

If only our passion to understand the other person were as great as our passion to be understood. Were this so, all of our apologies would be truly meaningful and healing.

CHAPTER 5

The Secret Life of
the Non-Apologizer

When I was researching the subject of apologies many years back, my nephew, Yarrow, was living in Japan and dating a Korean woman. In response to my queries, he wrote me the following about a major collision they'd had involving the matter of apologizing:

> *In the aftermath of an agonizing conversation, full of sundry twists, turns and accusations, she told me that she has never, not once apologized to her mother, father or a lover (!) For us, used to invoking the apology even for things completely outside our control, and forged by parents and teachers who demanded stand-up formal apologies, and it better be sincere, the fact that she'd never apologized grated.*

My nephew learned that for his Korean girlfriend, an apology signified social distance, and belonged in formal settings or in public life. For her, intimacy and apologies were incongruent:

> *Seems like the Korean idea (yes, I dare generalize from one woman to an entire culture) is that, to the degree our relationship is intimate, we don't need to apologize. Of course the person will forgive us, and of course they can read the non-verbal signs of apology, and of course they know the non-apologizer recognizes their own wrong and will try not to do it again. Well, it's good to know.*

It *is* good to know. Some cultural groups place a high premium on apologies and forgiveness. Others do not. Nor do we need to be born across the ocean from the other person to face the challenge of differences. Every relationship is a cross-cultural experience of sorts because we all view reality through different filters, and certain of these filters can give rise to a pretty unyielding stance.

OUR FIRST FAMILY

Consider the culture of our family of origin, one of our most important blueprints for how we navigate relationships. If we've been shamed as children, we may have an especially difficult time tolerating the adult experience of being wrong. Simply acknowledging a mistake with the requisite "I'm sorry" can boot us back to the unbearable experience of childhood shame.

Families also have their own "traditions" about giving and receiving apologies. If we grew up in a family where the adults didn't apologize when we needed them to, and almost never said, "I'm sorry, I was wrong," it may be difficult to forge a different pattern for ourselves. Or, alternatively, we may have grown up in a family where apologies were too big a deal, and when we said "I'm sorry" our apology was questioned rather than accepted at face value. If our efforts to apologize left us feeling worse, we may prefer as adults to avoid the entire process.

One man I saw in therapy, Geoffrey, was allergic to apologizing to anyone. "My parents were always in my face to get me to apologize to my brother, and they always assumed everything was my fault. They would say, 'Now, you apologize to Scott right now!' Then, 'That wasn't a real apology. Do it again and say it like you mean it!' "

Geoffrey found the whole process humiliating and confusing. Even worse were those incidents when his father behaved badly and then proceeded to apologize to Geoffrey in the most burdensome way imaginable. "My dad would lose it, and scream at me with such rage that I thought he might hit me, though he never did. Later he'd come and find me, and he'd be all weepy about how he had behaved. When he was drinking he had this pleading way of asking me to forgive him, as if I was supposed to hug and comfort him. That part felt as bad as his screaming."

Geoffrey's solution as an adult was to never say he was sorry. It didn't help that Geoffrey was married to someone for whom apologies mattered a great deal, and who vigorously demanded them, only to proclaim them worthless because she only received one when she insisted he give it.

WHAT'S YOUR PERSONAL VIEW?

People hold strikingly different views about how, when, and if to offer (and accept) apologies. "I don't apologize and I don't accept apologies," a friend tells me flatly. "When people apologize to me, they're trying to silence my anger. They're really saying, 'Look, I apologized, so be quiet already. Drop it.'" My friend views apologies as a manipulative tool to silence or placate the other person and to grab the moral high ground.

Some apologies are, indeed, motivated by nothing more than a wish to shut down the conversation and avoid further criticism—or they are used as an excuse to continue unfair or irresponsible behavior. That said, I have a different view. I believe that tendering an apology, one that is authentic and genuinely felt, helps the other person to feel validated, soothed, and cared for and can restore a sense of well-being and integrity to the one who sincerely feels she or he did something wrong. Without the possibility of apology and repair, the inherently flawed experience of being human would feel impossibly tragic.

Our beliefs about apologies are rooted in family and culture, and may be generations in the making.

When we explore these beliefs away from the heat of conflict, we can see how well they are working for us and modify them if necessary. Geoffrey, for example, did figure out in therapy how to offer apologies that reflected his personal values and best thinking, rather than staying stuck in a "Don't hold your breath waiting for an apology from *me!*" stance.

REAL MEN DON'T APOLOGIZE

Perhaps the number one risk factor for being a non-apologizer is being born male, just as the number one risk factor for being an over-apologizer is being born female. Research suggests that more men than women just won't go there when it comes to apologizing—a finding that holds true across cultures.

Most parents don't intentionally set out to raise their sons to be a James Bond or a man-of-steel-type figure, but none of us is entirely free of gender stereotypes. While feminism has challenged our old gender roles, they remain very much with us. "Be a man!" I recently heard a dad tell his eight-year-old son who was sobbing on the soccer field. I hadn't heard these words in a while, but every kid knows what it means to man up: *Be strong, don't cry, don't be too soft, sensitive, or vulnerable, don't be a sissy . . . in a word, don't be like a girl.* In contrast, the command to "Be a woman!" has no meaning at all, although the dictate to "Be a lady!" is perfectly clear.

We continue to shame boys for half of their humanity,

which we label "feminine." Our sons still grow up having to prove their masculinity over and over again to other men, often in the form of achieving status, dominance, and financial success. For some men, the very act of apologizing, of simply saying, "I was wrong, I made a mistake, I'm sorry," may feel uncomfortable, if not intolerable. As one man put it, "It makes me feel weak to apologize. It's like losing something and giving the other person the superior edge. And once you let your guard down, the other person can take advantage of you."

A poem by Rudyard Kipling captures a vision of masculinity that is still prominent in much of our society today:

> *If neither foes nor loving friends can hurt you,*
> *If all men count with you, but none too much;*
> *If you can fill the unforgiving minute*
> *With sixty seconds' worth of distance run,*
> *Yours is the Earth and everything that's in it,*
> *And—which is more—you'll be a Man, my son!*

The truth of the matter is quite different. If your loving friends can't hurt you, and if no one counts too much, you're flatly out of connection with yourself and with others. And if you have to fill the difficult minutes with the "distance run," you'll never sit still long enough to notice the disconnection, nor will you have an authentic center to even begin to think about how your behavior hurts or diminishes others. This "manly" way of being in the world does not lend itself to offering a heartfelt apology when an apology is due.

THE PROBLEM WITH PERFECTIONISM

While *more* men than women have difficulty apologizing, any particular man may apologize more easily than any particular woman. In my marriage, for example, Steve offers apologies a bit more easily than I do. And some women seem to embody Kipling's vision. No one is immune to becoming defensive and shutting down when our favored image of our self is challenged.

Some people are so hard on themselves for the mistakes they make that they don't have the emotional room to apologize to others—or at least not in the particularly vulnerable area (say, work or parenting) in which their self-esteem is most at stake. An example is my long-distance work relationship with a super-competent colleague whom I love and respect. She does not, however, apologize for any error that she makes, large or small, in the arena of work.

Recently she and I set up a ten-thirty morning phone meeting to discuss our joint participation in a workshop. Our phone meeting was scheduled for Tuesday, but she called Monday, and when she didn't reach me she texted, emailed, and left messages on my two other numbers, saying, "Harriet, where ARE you?" in a tone that failed to mask her irritation that I wasn't available.

A few hours later, when I had the chance, I sent her a short email saying our phone appointment was for the following day. She emailed back one word, "Right."

This incident would hardly be worth noting except that in our very long collegial relationship, she has never apologized, nor do I ever recall her saying something like, "Oops, my mistake." Or, "Aaiiii . . . I don't know what I was thinking." Or, "I got that wrong." Because I'm a person who easily apologizes for my mistakes in work situations, it's been hard for me to comprehend her inability to acknowledge and apologize for simple errors.

She offers her "perfectionism" as an explanation for her defensiveness. Knowing her as I do, I agree with her self-diagnosis. Perfectionism can, indeed, make it difficult for any of us to offer a simple apology, because we are unlikely to be able to view our errors and limitations in a light and self-loving way. While some perfectionistic people are prone to over-apologizing, the opposite occurs just as frequently.

When we adopt an attitude of terminal seriousness about our mistakes—or we equate mistakes with being unworthy, lesser, or bad—it's more difficult to admit error and apologize for being wrong. A vicious cycle ensues because the inability to admit error, orient to reality, and offer a heartfelt apology only leaves the perfectionist feeling less authentic and whole, that is, even "less perfect," which then further heightens the resistance to apologizing.

A MATTER OF SELF-WORTH

The perfectionist walks a tightrope above a canyon of low self-esteem. People who need to have it "all together" are in touch with their competence, but lose sight of the fact that we are all error-prone, imperfect human beings. It may therefore feel too risky to admit to error or wrongdoing, even to oneself. Perfectionists fail to identify with the wise words of Elizabeth Kübler-Ross: "I'm not okay, you're not okay, and *that's* okay."

To offer a serious apology, you need the inner strength to allow yourself to feel vulnerable. You need to be in touch with both your competence and your limitations. When you have fairly solid self-esteem you can admit to being in the wrong, without feeling like you're weakening the fabric of the self, or losing something to the other person.

In my work as a therapist, I've heard countless theories that my clients put forth about that person in their lives who won't step up to the apology plate. Here's a brief sampling. Each of these explanations is a bit different, but each speaks to the same essential theme of shaky self-esteem:

> *"God forbid my sister would apologize for being wrong, because she makes a show of being a perfect person with the perfect life. She once had a shame attack because I came to visit one afternoon and she was napping. Underneath, I think she feels lousy about herself."*

"My supervisor is so insecure that apologizing would make him feel like the wolf who bares his neck to his attacker as an admission of defeat, like he's lost his status in the group hierarchy."

"My husband is so controlling and rigid that when he's criticized he goes into debate mode, turns things around, and makes it the other person's fault."

"There's no way my brother is ever going to apologize to his wife because he feels so inadequate in her eyes. It would only give her more ammunition to criticize him and look down on him."

People's sense of self-worth is pivotal to their ability to look clearly at the hurt they've caused. The more solid one's sense of self-regard, the more likely that that person can feel empathy and compassion for the hurt party, and apologize from an authentic center.

THE UNBEARABLE WEIGHT OF SHAME

Nothing devastates self-worth like the experience of shame—the feeling of being essentially flawed, inadequate, and out of the flow of human connection. While guilt evokes true remorse and signals us to apologize, shame does the opposite. Brené Brown's work on shame and vulnerability has helped countless men and women identify the mischief of this emotion— and courageously speak, act, and show up in spite of it.

Shame and guilt are distinctly different emotions. Guilt is what we feel when we behave in a way that violates our core values and beliefs—assuming, of course, that our conscience is in good working order. The experience of guilt is usually tied to specific behaviors that we're not especially proud of, like betraying a friend's confidence, or hurting someone in the name of honesty.

Healthy guilt is to be distinguished from the non-productive guilt that women have long been encouraged to cultivate like a little flower garden—the kind of guilt that keeps women saying "I'm sorry" for no good reason at all. Healthy guilt is "good guilt." It's what inspires us to apologize when we stray from being the kind, honest, responsible person we aim to be—that is, when we deserve to be sorry.

Unlike healthy guilt, the experience of shame goes beyond specific behaviors to what a friend describes as "a yuck, poisoned feeling" about one's fundamental self. While guilt is about *doing*, shame is about *being*. Deep down we believe that another person couldn't possibly love or respect us if he or she really knew the whole, pitiful, god-awful truth about us.

To guard against the intolerable feeling of shame, we may fold ourselves up and hide in the darkest corner. We may apologize for taking up too much space or for using up too much of the valuable oxygen in the room. Or we may do the opposite and flip shame into contempt, arrogance, a need to control, and displays of one-upmanship, dominance, and superiority.

In the latter case the person may be hell-bent on not apologizing to anybody.

The overly apologetic style is more predominant in women, and the dominating style is more predominant in men, although there are many exceptions to this generalization. While these two styles of shame-avoidance look as different as night and day, they are flip sides of the same low-self-esteem coin. It took me a long time to fully appreciate that the person who feels essentially superior is no different than the person who feels essentially inferior. In both cases it will be challenging for the shame-based person to apologize wisely and well.

For an individual to look squarely at his or her harmful actions and to become genuinely accountable, that person must have a platform of self-worth to stand on. Only from the vantage point of this higher ground can people who have hurt others gain perspective and access empathy and remorse. Only from there can they look out at their less-than-honorable behaviors and apologize. Of course, a heartfelt apology cannot right a serious wrong, but it can be a first step.

WHY THE WORST OFFENDERS DON'T FEEL SORRY

Many decades ago in San Francisco, I administered psychological testing to a minister who had had sexual intercourse with each of his four daughters. He expressed no guilt or remorse. A religious man with "strong family values," he insisted that he did not want his daughters to be introduced to sexuality by strangers who might exploit them. I will never forget the burst of self-righteous anger that the father directed toward me when I asked him if he had initiated any sexual activity with his only son. "Dr. Lerner," he said, rising from his chair and almost spitting my name, "*that* would be a sin!"

How do we understand people who do great harm and feel no remorse? We might assume that such people are psychopaths to begin with, and lack any capacity to feel love, or to empathize with the people they harm. That is true for some. The man I described, although in many ways ordinary, engaged in a type of violence that few parents can even imagine. But, that said, the human capacity for self-deception is extraordinary.

The worse the offense and the greater the shame, the more difficult it is for the wrongdoer to empathize with the harmed party and feel remorse. Instead one tells oneself, "It wasn't my fault," or "I couldn't help myself," or "It's not that big a deal." Self-protective explanations often shift the blame onto the harmed party as ever deeper levels of self-deception come into play. One tells oneself, "She really asked for it," "I did it for his own good," or "It was necessary," and even "It never happened."

Whether the context is personal or political, all of us can create layers of defensiveness when we cannot face the shame of having violated our values and having harmed others. It is always easier to offer a sincere apology for small things than for serious transgressions.

When our identity and sense of worth are at risk of being diminished or annihilated, we will not be able to offer a true apology and face all that the challenge of earning back trust entails. We are more likely to wrap ourselves in a blanket of rationalization, minimization, and denial in order to survive. Defensiveness is no longer merely a roadblock that we can observe and get past after we calm down and limber up the thinking part of our brain. When we have lost sight of our value and worth, defensiveness is where we live.

SHAMING THE SHAMER DOESN'T WORK

When faced with an unrepentant wrongdoer who won't apologize and feels no remorse, it's a normal human impulse to blame the blamer and shame the shamer. The problem is that it doesn't help—not with simple offenses or with very serious ones. Smacking labels and diagnoses on nonrepentant offenders only rigidifies their defenses rather than opening their hearts.

It's not just an expression of the offender's pathological denial that he or she doesn't want to accept the label of "a batterer," "an abuser," or "a toxic parent." The refusal to take on an identity defined by our worst deeds is a healthy act of resistance. If one's identity as a person is equated with one's worst acts, it can be impossible to accept responsibility or access genuine feelings of sorrow and remorse. To do so would destroy whatever remnants of self-worth a person had left.

As a therapist who has worked with serious offenders, I have helped men and women to resist the notion that their crime defines them. In treatment, a person can have the opportunity to begin to remember and share incidents in his life where he believed, felt, or acted in ways he could identify as good and honorable, whether as a son, brother, husband, neighbor, or breadwinner. Only by enlarging the offender's platform of self-worth might that person find his way to empathize with the pain the hurt party feels, apologize in a heartfelt way, and work to ensure that it will never happen again.

We have the best chance to reach people who do serious harm in treatment programs that do not label them as bad or sick, but rather enhance self-respect while accepting no excuses for violent behavior. When one has physically harmed another person, the words "I'm sorry" are obviously not enough. More is required. The offending party may do jail time, public service, or meaningful volunteer work. One man I worked with who had hit his wife worked Saturday mornings and gave the money to a safe house for women, as part of his desire to show his wife how seriously he took his past out-of-control behavior.

Once we label and shame people ("He is a sexual predator"), we narrow the possibility of redemption and positive change. A heartfelt apology for serious wrongdoings can only be offered by those who can see their mistakes as part of being human, and who can hold on to a big picture of their multifaceted, ever-changing self. Labeling and demonizing the offender will not open their minds, soften their hearts, and break through their defenses. It will do the opposite.

"HE HAD A TERRIBLE CHILDHOOD" AND OTHER POOR EXCUSES

While shaming isn't useful, neither is it useful to allow the wrongdoer to rely on excuses and psychological rationalizations. If we view the offending party as one who has no agency, choice, or will, he loses the opportunity to be truly accountable for his behavior. This is true for the youngest bully or the most seasoned criminal.

A *New Yorker* cartoon by Bob Mankoff shows a woman on the witness stand saying, *"I know he cheated on me because of his childhood abuse, but I shot him because of mine."* The cartoon drives home the point that psychological explanations aren't helpful when they invite people to avoid being responsible for the harmful consequences of their decisions and actions.

The wrongdoer cannot maintain honor and dignity when denied agency and allowed to rely on excuses and psychological rationalizations. While we need to consider how the past and the present affect behavior, a difficult personal history or painful current circumstance doesn't *cause* a person to behave badly.

Most people who have suffered a traumatic past or horrific present do not go on to harm others. Instead, many such people become loving parents and good citizens—adults who develop gifts that benefit us all.

AN IMPORTANT MESSAGE TO THE HARMED PARTY

The most urgent issues—those where we feel most desperate to be heard and understood—pertain to violations of trust by people we have most relied on. Often, in my work as a therapist, the harmed party wants to confront the wrongdoer, frequently a parent or other family member, in the hope of receiving a heartfelt apology—one that would include a clear acknowledgment of harm that was disregarded at the time, and validation for the fact that certain events or communications occurred and were emotionally damaging.

Instead of the longed-for outcome, the harmed party may end up feeling re-traumatized. Most people who commit serious harm never get to the point where they can admit to their harmful actions, much less apologize and aim to repair them. Their shame leads to denial and self-deception that overrides their ability to orient toward reality. No person can be more honest with us than they can be with their own self.

Before you open up a conversation with a person who has harmed you, keep in mind that protecting yourself comes first. Reduce your expectations to zero for getting the response you want and deserve. Speak your truths because you need to speak for your own self—because this is the ground you want to stand on, irrespective of whatever response you receive. A heartfelt apology is unlikely to be forthcoming, now or ever.

No individual will feel accountable and genuinely remorseful—no matter how well you communicate—if doing so threatens to define him or her in an intolerable way. The other person's willingness to own up to harmful deeds has nothing to do with how much she or he does or doesn't love you. Rather, the capacity to take responsibility, feel empathy and remorse, and offer a meaningful apology rests on how much *self*-love and *self*-respect that person has available. We don't have the power to bestow these traits on anyone but ourselves.

CHAPTER 6

"He's So Defensive!"
What Do *You*
Have to Do With It?

Some folks are entrenched non-apologizers, and there's no changing that. They are too defensive, too covered in shame, and can't or won't see themselves objectively. They will never own up.

Often, however, the challenge of apology and reconciliation is a dance that takes place between at least two people, and varies according to context and circumstance. This means that if you aren't getting the apology you need and deserve, you may unwittingly be contributing to the problem. Needless to say, no one who is suffering and has a legitimate grievance wants to hear this. Yet we need to.

You can't *make* another person drop the defensiveness and fess up. Nor are you responsible for the wrongdoer's failure to apologize when she or he should. You can, however, avoid adding to that individual's defensiveness, so that you have the best chance of exceeding his threshold of deafness and being heard.

Few of us have family and friends in our lives who are as dedicated and heroic listeners as Katherine (Chapter 4) was with her daughter. If you confront the other person in an angry or critical way, it may take only a nanosecond before the other person's "But, but, but . . ." response kicks in and you've lost them.

Even if the apology we seek concerns a relatively small matter, the wrongdoer will get more defensive if you overstate your case or come on too strong. How you navigate your part of the relationship with a defensive person matters, so keep the following ideas in mind.

STICK TO THE FACTS

People won't apologize if they're feeling overly accused or pushed to assume more than their fair share of the blame. As one man put it, "When my wife criticizes me, I don't want to apologize because I feel like I'm putting my head on the chopping block. If I apologize, I'm agreeing with her that I'm the whole problem, which isn't true."

Even a slight exaggeration of the facts can kick up the other person's defensiveness. If your partner came home late from work six times last month, and you accuse him of coming home late eight times, he'll likely focus on correcting the facts, rather than taking in your legitimate complaint.

Consider the following fragment of conversation between one couple in my consulting room:

HE: *You were rude and critical all morning and I'm most irritated by the fact that you didn't even think it was necessary to apologize.*

SHE: *All morning? How many times was I actually rude to you?*

HE: *About seven times.*

SHE: *I was rude three times. [She has counted, and she now approaches him like a trial lawyer.] You think seven? I want you to tell me each of the seven times I was rude to you. Be specific.*

HE: *I don't care how many times you were rude. It's not acceptable, and what really is obnoxious is that you act like you can just be rude and then ignore it like it didn't happen.*

SHE: *So why do you have to exaggerate? Why can't you say that I've been rude three times? Why don't you apologize for exaggerating?*

Anyone who is criticized inaccurately will listen defensively. When we listen defensively we automatically focus on the exaggerations, distortions, and inaccuracies that indeed may be there, rather than listen for the essence of what's being said. Then we may swing into debate mode to correct the facts. Once in debate mode, an apology feels like losing.

When a Banana's Not Just a Banana

I demonstrate my worst overdoing behavior in my marriage. Steve is right there on the scene and the one with whom I'm least likely to watch myself. Who can blame me for taking life's stresses out on him? After all, what's a partner for?

When Steve recently came home from our local co-op with five bananas, all at the same level of ripeness, I immediately confronted him. There are only two of us in the house, we're not huge banana eaters, neither of us makes banana bread, and I thought he should be down on his knees with remorse because we've talked about the "banana thing" several times before.

I was already in a bad mood and having a low-self-esteem day. I leapt from the facts (we'd have to gorge on bananas or at least three would end up in the compost bin) to below-the-belt tactics ("What kind of person doesn't care about letting food rot when people go hungry?") and concluded with that most supportive of all questions: "What's *wrong* with you?" I then demanded an apology, along with his word, written in stone, that the banana thing would never happen again.

"I don't want to hear about it," Steve said with open

irritation. "You do the shopping yourself if you're going to criticize how I do it." I argued back and then stomped off because, well, why am *I* suddenly the bad guy? After all, I would *never* buy five bananas at the same level of ripeness, which obviously makes me the better world citizen and more highly evolved human being. And why was Steve so defensive about his obvious screw-up? He should feel fortunate to receive my constructive corrections and criticisms.

If you want to invite the other person to consider his behavior and offer an apology, remember the most basic rule of good communication. Criticize the *behavior*, not the *person*. But under the sway of strong emotions we may automatically ramp up the intensity. It took me all of ten seconds to leap from the facts (buying five ripe bananas meant three would rot) to questioning what sort of person would do such a thing. Paradoxically, it's in our most enduring and important relationships that we're least likely to be our most mature and thoughtful selves.

Overdoing It Can Be Subtle

Sometimes overdoing a criticism is hard to spot because it's subtle. We may be holding the other person responsible not only for their behavior, but also for our reaction to it. My friend Bob told me this story:

> *My home office has been a mess lately, and Jill, who shares the space, is a much more organized person than I am.*

After glancing at the stacks of papers everywhere on my desk and floor, she said to me: "When I walk into this room, I feel like our household is totally falling apart." Totally falling apart! Our household? I'm her hardworking faithful partner of fourteen years and because my half of the office is a mess, she feels like everything is crumbling around her? And yet when I said, "That's a pretty extreme statement," she simply responded, "Well, it's how I feel."

Bob picked up his papers from the floor, but didn't muster up the maturity to apologize. As he put it, "The accusation was simply too much." Despite Jill's attempt to couch it in "I-language," it was a broad condemnation in both content and tone. From Jill's perspective, she was sharing her feelings. But Bob felt like he was being held responsible not only for his messiness, but also for her feeling like their household was falling apart. This made it more difficult for him to apologize for his inconsiderate behavior. He cleaned up his mess, but felt more like the victim than the inconsiderate one.

SAY IT SHORTER!

Here's an incredibly important principle for the hurt or angry party that is simple to understand in theory, but difficult to put into practice. *Say it shorter.*

If you're trying to get through to a non-apologizer— or any difficult or defensive person—keep in mind that overtalking on your part will lead to underlistening from the other. This is true whether the offense you're addressing is large or small.

People take in very little information when they don't want to hear what you're saying. If you go on too long, you're actually protecting the other person from taking in your anger or pain, because that person will shut down and vacate the emotional premises. He or she won't have the space to sit with what you've said and to consider the valid point you may be making. It doesn't matter how old or young that other person happens to be.

When I was conducting informal research for my book *The Mother Dance,* I asked children in family sessions to tell me one thing that their mother or father could do to make the family better. "Say it shorter, Mom!" was the most common response, or, "You tell me I have to be more responsible, Dad, and then you go on and on for so long about it that I can't even remember the first thing you said."

I can relate. I remember lecturing my younger son, Ben, during his senior year in high school about his failure to clean up his mess in the room where he watched television. I'd go on and on even though his eyes were rolling back in his head, his brain waves were flat, and I clearly didn't have his attention.

If your intention is to be heard and to make room for a sincere apology and behavioral change, opt for brevity. This is especially challenging if your automatic tendency is to say too much. Here's a snapshot of my own inclination to overtalk things when I'm aiming

to convince the other person of "the truth" of his misguided ways.

Why Can't He Just Say Thank You?

I've known Alan for more than thirty years, and when
I'm in his hometown of Chicago I take him out to dinner. I used to go there for work, and had the luxury of
using my publisher's credit card to pay for our meal.
I'd plunk down the credit card and say something like,
"Let's toast to my generous publisher!" We were, after
all, dining in the best restaurants, and Alan had a taste
for fine wines. We'd clink wineglasses and I'd note that
he never joined me in saying, "Thank you," or even,
"Great that your publisher is picking up the tab."

This didn't really bother me until I began paying
for the meals out of my own pocket, a fact that I didn't
hesitate to gracefully slip into the conversation when
the check arrived. Given the disparity in our incomes,
I understood that Alan might expect that I'd pay, but
I found myself feeling increasingly resentful that he
never expressed a word of appreciation. How could it
be so difficult for a person to say thank you?

I wanted to talk with him about it, yet I felt hesi-
tant to do so. Alan is not a particularly open person,
and since we saw each other infrequently it would be
difficult to repair whatever bad feeling one or both of
us might be left with. Nor was I comfortable, given he
lived on the economic edge, to suggest that we split
the check.

I was sharing my dilemma on a phone call with my son Matt, who has a unique talent for saying difficult things with a clarity, directness, and lightness that I've long admired. He doesn't overtalk things, nor does he have the slightest edge in his voice when expressing a different or difficult point of view. It's a style that allows him to bring out the best in the people that he manages in the workplace.

"What's your goal?" Matt asked, in response to my seeking his opinion about whether I should speak up or forever hold my peace. "What do you want to accomplish?"

"I want Alan to feel awful about himself," I replied.

"That's not very mature of you," Matt said, laughing.

"Well, it's true."

Sure, I wanted Alan to apologize and to say he was sorry and make it a point to always say thank you from that day forward. But I also wanted Alan to think about his bad manners and lack of gratitude and to feel wildly embarrassed and remorseful for at least as much time as I had wasted ruminating about his rude behavior, and maybe longer.

"What would you say to him?" Matt asked.

I responded with something like the following:

Alan, I've been wanting to talk to you about something for a very long time. I always pick up the check when we eat out and that's okay because I can afford to. But it really bothers me that you don't say thank you, that you've never once said thank you or expressed any appreciation at all. I've tried over the years to make sense of this and I really can't. When my publisher was picking up the tab, I thought, "Okay, you apparently don't think you need to thank my publisher, although it still would have been nice if you had showed some gratitude." But the same behavior continued when you knew I was paying. I mean, you never, ever once thanked me. Maybe you think that you don't need to thank people who make more money than you do, although I don't have as much money as I think you think I have. Or maybe you just feel entitled to people paying your way because you've had difficult times economically. But I have to tell you that it feels lousy when the check comes and I take out my credit card and you literally sit there mute. It also seems ironic that you apparently don't consider this behavior rude, because you are a pretty fussy guy, and you can get hypercritical about the smallest details of propriety, like how people dress for an occasion, or how they set the table for a dinner party. So I'm hoping you can explain your behavior to me because I don't get it and, like I said, it really bothers me. And, of course, I'd appreciate an apology, but I don't imagine I'll get one because I know that people who can't say "Thank you" are very unlikely to say "I'm sorry."

I went on for what might add up to a few paragraphs longer before I ran out of steam.

There was silence on the other end of the phone. I sounded pathetic, even to myself.

"So what would *you* say, Matt?" I asked.

Matt's answer was a tad more succinct.

"Alan, when I pick up the check, I'd really like you to say thank you."

Why Less Is More

Hearing Matt's one-sentence reply out loud drove home the wisdom of it. A one-line request for a behavior change would give Alan the best chance of thinking about his failure to thank me, and apologizing for his bad manners. My lecture, or even the first fifteen seconds of it, would have only ramped up his defensiveness.

When we believe we won't get through to the offending party, we often increase the intensity and lengthen our arguments. This does not help—and usually hurts. We may not recognize that our tone of voice or the sheer number of sentences may be the culprit. Despite a lifetime of bad results, many people keep believing that the more details they include in their efforts to get through, the more the other person will see the irrefutable truth of their point and realize the extent of the hurt they have caused.

I haven't done a large-scale study, but my observations suggest that the higher the word count on an emotionally loaded subject, the faster the other person shuts down. Try the experiment of saying a criticism in three sentences or less to the offending party, and leave it at that: "I want you to say thank you when I drive you places," or "You forgot to take the garbage out for the second week in a row," or "I feel uncomfortable about how much you drank at the party. Then you were rude to my mother, and that's not acceptable." Keep the edge out of your voice, because intensity and reactivity will only lead to more of the same.

Obviously, longer conversations are necessary on many subjects to repair a disconnection and to let the other person understand the full measure of your anger or pain. But these important conversations will go better if you practice brevity on the smaller things.

SOMETIMES YOU NEED TO LOSE IT TO GET THROUGH

Generally speaking, you'll have a better chance of reaching the wrongdoer if you approach him at a time when you are feeling calm—preferably at a moment when you actually are *liking* that person. I used to believe that timing and tact were the opposite of honesty. In fact, the opposite is true. Timing and tact, along with kindness, are exactly what make honesty possible with the most difficult and defensive individuals.

That said, there are certain times when only a raw expression of your emotions will break through the other person's defensiveness and exceed his or her threshold of deafness. Important addendum: This will happen only if your outburst comes as a big surprise to both of you, meaning it's a rare event and not the rule.

Heading Off an Affair

A therapy client of mine, Kathy, discovered her husband, a lecturer in a local college, was having an emotional affair with one of his graduate students. Some instinct led her to go into the "deleted" box of his email, where she found his provocative and sexualized messages. He wrote, for example, "I didn't dare hug you when you left my office Monday, because I didn't trust that I'd be able to stop myself there." It seemed that they hadn't (yet) had sex.

My client confronted him immediately, and they had endless conversations about the situation. My client said all the right things and expressed the whole range of feelings that were evoked by reading the emails. She took a clear position on what she expected from her husband and how much he was putting at risk if he didn't stop the flirtation. Probably she said all that could be said. Her husband said that he was sorry, that he'd change his behavior. He brought her flowers and asked for forgiveness.

Kathy was a therapist herself, and she talked like one. She felt it was important to take a position calmly, to speak in "I-language," and to keep the intensity down so as to ensure her message was heard. The problem was that Kathy almost always talked this way. She was, by nature, a very low-key person who didn't have much dynamic range in her speaking style. Teasingly, her younger sister sometimes called her "one-note Kathy."

One evening in their bedroom when her husband seemed distant and preoccupied, Kathy simply lost it. She began screaming at him about the graduate student. "It was the kind of screaming that left my vocal cords raw," Kathy told me. "I was afraid I might have actually damaged them." After she screamed, for maybe a few minutes or less, she threw herself down on the floor of their small bedroom closet, sobbing uncontrollably, refusing her husband's pleas to come out or at least open the closet door. She slept in another room that night.

This episode got through to Kathy's husband in a way that all the previous conversation had not. The rawness of Kathy's emotional response opened his heart in a way that his wife's calm, "I-language" and "good communication" had never done. "Losing it," to use Kathy's term, turned out to be both good and, perhaps more to the point, unavoidable. Her husband backed up his apology with appropriate action, which, of course, is what gives an apology its meaning.

When "losing it" is a very rare and surprising departure from your usual style—and does not harm the other person—a raw show of emotion may get through to the wrongdoer at a deeper level.

SHAMING NEVER HELPS

I recently overheard a mother disciplining a child who had taken a fistful of sweets off the shelves of a local supermarket and stuffed it in his jacket pocket, only to be discovered upon leaving the premises. The conversation began well. The mother said, "It's wrong to take something that isn't yours. It's also against the law. Let's go back inside the store and you can apologize for taking the sweets."

When her son said nothing, however, the mother quickly moved from criticizing his behavior (what he *did*) to attacking his character (who he *was*). "I cannot *believe* you did this! I always thought that you were an honest boy and now I can't trust you. I am so disappointed in you." The boy was probably all of seven.

"I'm sorry," the boy said, head down, eyes averted. Shaming people—whether they are seven or seventy—may indeed force an apology, but that apology is likely to be motivated by the wish to escape the intolerable feeling of being shamed. A shamed person wants to fold up and disappear, so an apology becomes a quick way to exit the situation.

You can shame someone into saying they are sorry with a one-liner, because shame is *that* powerful. If you shame someone in a lesser position of power, it can lead that person to conform, obey, and give the obligatory apology. But shame will not inspire reflection, self-observation, and personal growth. These are essentially self-loving tasks that do not flourish in an atmosphere of self-depreciation and self-blame.

One of my favorite *Peanuts* cartoons shows Charlie Brown consulting with Lucy at her five-cents psychiatrist booth. "The trouble with you, Charlie Brown," she says, "is that you're you." What is Charlie Brown to do with *that*? We can apologize for what we *do*. We cannot apologize for who we *are*.

When we go from criticizing specific behaviors to taking a hatchet to someone's already rickety self-worth, we narrow the possibility that they will be able to consider their harmful behavior, feel empathy and remorse, and be motivated to make amends. Shaming will also fundamentally harm your relationship with the other person, even if the damage doesn't show up till many years later.

WHO IS RESPONSIBLE FOR WHAT?
A TRICKY ANGER QUESTION

The process of apology and repair gets muddled when we lose clarity about "Who is responsible for what?" If you're the hurt or angry party, aim to be as clear-eyed as possible about the part that each person plays in the complex dance of relationships—your own self included. It's not easy to sort out.

Recall the story of the mother who asked Matt to apologize for her son banging his head on the wooden floor (Chapter 2). This example may have struck you as extreme, but confusion about "Who is responsible for what?" permeates our relationships. When tempers flare, it's especially difficult to sort this out, and we make the mistake of blaming one person for the behavior of both.

A CLASSIC CONFUSION—
WITH THANKS TO HANSEL AND GRETEL

A client tells me, "My dad's new wife is so controlling. He can't even call me from their house. We have to talk when he's at work." It doesn't occur to her that her father is responsible for protecting their relationship, and that he can choose to lovingly and firmly tell his wife that he needs to be in charge of where and when he calls his daughter. When we're not clear about who is responsible for what, we won't be clear about who is accountable for their less-than-sterling behavior, who owes whom the apology, and who needs to back that apology with a change in behavior.

Consider our time-honored fairy tale *Hansel and Gretel*. Here the wicked stepmother is blamed for the father's decision to send his own son and daughter out into the woods to die. Parenting is a sacred pact and these children are *his* primary responsibility. But oh, well, how could the poor guy help himself, when his wife was such a meanie?

When Hansel and Gretel grow up (I'm moving them off the page and into real life now), they will carry the buried knowledge that their father abandoned them. But their unconscious loyalty to their only parent, and their wish to protect this bond, will leave them no room to think clearly and hold their father accountable. The stepmother is likely to remain the lightning rod that absorbs all their anger, unless the father—perhaps with the help of the kind therapist who lives in the forest nearby—can access his guilt and remorse for betraying his children. Only then would he have the opportunity to open a conversation with his children in which he expressed his profound sorrow for his earlier unconscionable behavior. Only then could he say, *"Yes, your stepmother was a piece of work, but the responsibility to stand up to her and protect you was one hundred percent mine. I abandoned you both, and put your lives at risk. I would give anything to be able to go back in time and give you the love and protection you both deserved. There is no excuse for what I did."*

Hansel and Gretel is a fairy tale whose message (wicked stepmother/innocent, beleaguered father) reflects a common confusion in family life. We target mothers-in-law, stepmoms, and daughters-in-law not only for their own difficult behavior (for which they are accountable) but also for the passive or distant behavior of our husbands, fathers, and sons. In this way we may avoid the challenge of holding the men in our lives responsible for having a voice, for managing their relationships with courage, clarity, and conviction. In lesbian and gay couples there is a similar tendency to blame our adult child's partner (or ex) for whatever mess he or she is making of things, rather than recognizing our son or daughter's part in the drama.

DID THE WRONGDOER "CAUSE" YOUR FEELINGS AND BEHAVIOR?

The other person is more likely to be accountable and to apologize when we are able to share our thoughts and feelings without holding that person responsible for causing them. This is what "I-language" is all about.

We *are* responsible for our own behavior. But we are not responsible for other people's reactions, nor are they responsible for ours. The difficult stepmother did not *cause* her husband to abandon his children. He had other options. Matthew did not *cause* his playmate's head-banging. One hopes this boy has since learned better ways to manage his anger and frustration.

We can all think of situations where one person's terrible behavior (a profound betrayal) is arguably responsible for causing the other person's reaction, and we are taught to view human transactions in simple cause-and-effect terms. But relationship systems typically don't operate in a simple linear fashion.

Consider the husband who has an ongoing love affair in a marriage where he has vowed to be monogamous. He is, indeed, responsible for his actions, which include not only whom he lies *with* (the affair partner) but also whom he lies *to* (his wife). The husband is the only one responsible for his deception. His wife did not *cause* the affair, whether through her emotional distance, readiness to criticize, sexual unavailability, chronic illness, or her thirty extra pounds. She may have contributed to the likelihood of an infidelity, but many husbands do not handle marital problems or any of life's other stresses by having affairs.

Now consider the reaction of the wife who discovers this terrible betrayal. Perhaps one woman becomes so depressed that she takes her life. Another woman leaves the marriage and avoids any possibility of future relationships, saying she will never be able to trust again. A third woman, post-divorce, happily remarries, with a man who is loving and responsible.

Did the unfaithful partner *make* the first wife commit suicide? Did he *cause* the second woman to never trust a man again? Was he *responsible* for the third woman feeling happier than ever before in her new marriage? We might even add a hypothetical fourth wife, who upon discovering the affair feels abject relief. "Now I can finally leave this guy," she tells herself, "and I don't have to worry about my parents blaming me for the divorce." Should her husband be credited for doing a good deed?

THE CHALLENGE OF DOUBLE VISION

When it comes to offering an apology vs. hoping to receive one, a bit of double vision is required to get it right.

If you are the person *offering* an apology, it is essential to speak the language of cause-and-effect, and to take unambiguous responsibility for the consequences of your actions and its impact on the other person. It is the only way to acknowledge the specific ways your actions have resulted in the other person's hurt or suffering. It would not fly, for example, for Kathy's husband to say, "I apologize for sexualizing the relationship with my graduate student. It was wrong. But don't hold me responsible for your anger and pain. Your feelings are your responsibility." That would be a sleazy, low-integrity apology.

When you are the harmed party, however, and you want the defensive person who hurt you to take responsibility for his or her behavior, you have a different challenge. Try sharing your reactions without holding the other person responsible for *causing* your feelings. There is greater clarity and self-empowerment in saying, "When I discovered what you did, I felt devastated and crazy," rather than, "You *made* me feel devastated and crazy."

A FINAL WORD OF ADVICE

Don't demand an apology. Requesting an apology is fine, but demanding one is counterproductive. On the couples front, psychologist Ellen Wachtel notes, "Demanding an apology can be harmful. Your partner may feel as if he or she is being asked to grovel. There is something humiliating about being forced to apologize on demand. It can make the apologizer feel like a child or like someone lacking in self-respect."

People do not respond well to being told how they should think, feel, or behave—and that includes being told to apologize. You'll have a better chance of getting through if you don't try to "make" the other person say they're sorry. And if the other person apologizes because you've demanded it, his or her words won't be sincerely felt. Instead, try to model the heartfelt, spontaneous apology that you would like to receive. And be generous in accepting the apology offered to you in good faith.

CHAPTER 7

How—and Whether— to Accept the Olive Branch

Once, after a long flight, I made my way along with my husband and two small boys to rent a car. The rental process was on hold and there were no available seats, so I sat down with the boys on the floor to wait next to our luggage while Steve got in line to see what was up.

I opened a small bag of nuts mixed with M&M's and offered them to Matt and Ben. There was an adorable little girl, about five years old, sitting next to me on the floor with her mother. She looked longingly at the treats and without thinking I offered her some as well. She happily grabbed a handful and gobbled it down.

About five minutes later, it occurred to me that I hadn't asked the girl's mother whether it was okay for me to offer the nuts and chocolate to her daughter. I initially put the thought out of mind, because the mother hadn't intervened and the incident quickly seemed like old news. But because the idea of apologizing kept coming back to me I decided to say something, even though I felt awkward doing so. I finally caught the mother's attention and said, "I'm sorry that I gave your daughter chocolate without asking you. I wasn't thinking and I want to apologize."

I was quite certain that she would say, "Oh, don't worry about it." Or, "No problem." Instead she looked me in the eyes and said, "Thank you for the apology. I appreciate it."

There was a quiet dignity in the way this mother accepted my apology, and what she *didn't* say was equally as important as her spoken words.

She didn't excuse or disqualify my apology in order to make the situation a bit more comfortable in the moment. She was mature enough to not have to protect me from my own feelings.

She didn't get angry or otherwise intense. There was no edge in her voice, no hint of resentment.

She didn't take the opportunity to instruct me, although she might have been tempted to. She didn't say, "Are you aware that my daughter could have been diabetic or allergic to nuts?" Or, "Did you think about the fact that your boys' dirty hands were just on the floor and then in that bag?"

It was just, "Thank you for the apology. I appreciate it." It was a clear, non-blaming, unambiguous acknowledgment that, yes, she agreed that I had done something to apologize for. Because she held the connection with her full presence, I have never forgotten this exchange or offered treats to another child without checking with a parent. I've also remembered this moment of someone accepting an apology with simplicity and grace.

IT TAKES COURAGE TO SAY
"THANK YOU FOR THE APOLOGY"

As trivial as this incident may sound, a surprising number of people have difficulty saying, "Thank you for the apology. I appreciate it."

Consider my friend who recently had a small party in which one guest, Frank, talked in endless detail about his recent trip to Italy, leaving little room for others to speak. The following morning, my friend called me and shared with great irritation how Frank had told story after story, hardly pausing to take a breath, and failing to ask a single question of anyone else.

To his credit, Frank called my friend later that day and apologized for being a "conversation hog" during the dinner. "When I thought about it, I was a bit embarrassed," he said. "I was going to send you an email, but I decided to call."

"Oh, no!" my friend responded without missing a beat. "There's no need to apologize. It was clear that you were very excited about the trip and we all loved hearing your stories."

Many of us dismiss apologies that the other person has gathered the courage to make for the same reason

my friend did. We want to end an uncomfortable moment as quickly as possible, even if this means telling
the person who is apologizing that it's nothing, no big
deal, and he shouldn't even think about it. Of course
he should and did think about, or else he wouldn't be
offering the apology.

If the other person has pushed through his or her
discomfort to do the right thing and apologize, we
can push through our discomfort and say, "Thanks for
the apology." It's important to resist the temptation to
cancel the effort at repair that a genuine apology is.

HOW TO TEACH YOUR CHILD TO APOLOGIZE

What's the best way to teach children to apologize?
I posed this question to a group of therapists, who
unanimously gave the same answer. The adults should
model the behavior they want children to learn. If you
don't offer a heartfelt apology to your child when it's
due, why should your son or daughter apologize to
you?

Modeling the behavior you want your children to
learn is undeniably a good idea. Your children are
watching you. Some parents feel reluctant to apologize to their kids because they think it undercuts their
authority and makes them look weak and uncertain.
Actually, it models a stronger approach to the world
that reflects a concern for fairness, and an ability to
orient to reality. It shows children that their parents
can admit to being wrong without being lesser people

for it. Indeed, the ability to apologize is one of the greatest gifts that we can give to our kids. Children have a strong sense of justice, and suffer when a parent's defensiveness invalidates what the child knows to be true.

My work with families leads me to suggest that there is an additional guideline for adults to follow if we want to teach children to apologize. *Learn to say, "Thank you for the apology," and stop there.* This piece of advice sounds simple but is difficult to put into practice. We reflexively use the apology as a springboard to say more.

When children apologize, they are likely to hear: *That's good that you apologized, but I want you to think more about how you made your brother feel when you excluded him from the game. Do you really feel sorry or are these just words you are saying? And maybe next time you'll consider apologizing to your brother before I have to ask you to do it.*

One eleven-year-old boy put it this way: "I hate to apologize because it always ends up feeling icky." He knows that in his family when he says "I'm sorry" his apology will invariably be followed by sermonizing about the importance of empathy, or a reminder that he's done this selfish, thoughtless thing before—or something will be said that makes him want to put his fingers in his ears and get away as quickly as possible.

Some adults negate the apologies of children in mind-bending ways. Consider this story a friend tells me about her child's fourth-grade classroom. Whenever a student misbehaves the teacher gives that person "the look." When the student apologizes she always replies, "If you were really sorry you wouldn't have done it."

This standard response isn't limited to repeat offenders in which case it might make some sense. The teacher's stern, disapproving look solicits an apology and recognition of the student's misbehavior, which she then immediately negates. My friend's daughter surely isn't the only child in the class confused by the teacher's response, which contradicts everything that apologizing and accepting apologies should be about.

Want to teach your child to apologize? Remember the woman at the airport. Make her your role model and accept your child's apology as she accepted mine. Of course there may be a need for further discussion, but it doesn't have to happen right then, in a way that dissolves the apology and makes the apologizer feel like, "What's the point?"

DON'T DISSECT THE OTHER PERSON'S APOLOGY WITH TALMUDIC PRECISION

It's laudable to examine our own apologies and hold them to a high standard. But holding others to these same standards is often counterproductive. Doing so may only serve to prolong a conflict and to keep a relationship stuck in distance and blame.

My friend Robert flew from Cleveland to New York to help his son, Aaron, move his small business to a new location. He returned home feeling wiped out and resentful. Part of the problem he recognized as his own. As a card-carrying overfunctioner and fix-it person, Robert had a long history of doing and giving more than he could comfortably do or give, then resenting the recipient of his efforts. Nevertheless, he felt bitter and resentful that Aaron appeared to take his efforts for granted. He told me that Aaron had never really thanked him, not in a way that was commensurate to the time and effort that Robert had put into helping with the move.

In the week following his return, Robert kept ruminating about his son's lack of gratitude and decided to call Aaron to let him know. Aaron seemed surprised. He said, "Really? I didn't thank you? Of course I appreciated all the work you did. I'm sorry."

His apology was rejected. "It felt like Aaron was just trying to placate me," Robert told me. "It sounded perfunctory, not at all sincere." So instead of saying, "Thanks for the apology," and leaving it there, Robert went on to criticize Aaron's "sense of entitlement." He told his son that he felt used and ended the call on an angry note, saying, "The next time you need to move, go hire a moving company."

Give the Other Person the Benefit of the Doubt

We can't always rank the other person's sincerity quotient when they tell us they're sorry, and it can be counterproductive to try to assess it. Anxiety or discomfort can make the apologizer sound robotic.

Plus it can take time to genuinely *feel* sorry when confronted with a complaint.

When I apologized at the airport for giving chocolate to the little girl, I wasn't feeling especially sorry, which was why I expected to hear, "Oh, it was nothing." My apology was sort of a halfhearted one. Only *after* the mother accepted my apology in the particular way that she did, did I actually begin to genuinely *feel* sorry and to consider how this mother might have felt. Also, nobody's going to feel especially sorry if we're labeling them entitled or narcissistic, or tossing any diagnosis or insult into the conversation.

The only test of the sincerity of Aaron's apology is whether he does a better job expressing gratitude for Robert's help the next time around. The sincerity test of an apology is in the follow-up. And, of course, Robert also needs to work on his own style of doing and giving more than he can comfortably do or give, and then resenting his son for "using" him.

I reminded Robert that accepting an apology needn't mean that all is resolved, or forgiven, or that there's no room for further discussion. Robert did call Aaron again, and apologized for being grumpy and out of line during the phone call. Robert's apology was accepted.

WORDS ARE NOT THE ONLY WAY TO SAY I'M SORRY

I'll never forget Marvin, a farmer who came grudgingly to therapy on his "doctor's orders" because he was depressed and irritable. His long-term marriage was at an impasse. When I asked him about how things were going at home, he told me that his wife, Bernice, wanted to put him out to pasture.

Marvin told me that he wasn't any good at being a husband. He shared, in the same tone he discussed the weather, many instances of not being there for Bernice. She had breast cancer surgery at the age of sixty-two, and the surgery was scheduled in the middle of harvest time. When she came out of the anesthesia to whatever news would be waiting for her—the good, bad, or terrible—he wasn't there. Marvin could handle a backbreaking workload on the farm, but showing up in tough emotional situations wasn't his strong suit. Bernice had long ago stopped expecting closeness from him, and she maintained her distance from him as well.

What motivates people to change is sometimes a mystery, but something shifted in Marvin during the time we were meeting together. He began telling me that Bernice was a good woman. He knew he had often let her down and that he had a lot to make up for. But there was no way he was going to apologize for his past behavior or bring it up for discussion. "What's done is done and words can't change it," Marvin told me. "I don't believe in apologizing and neither does Bernice."

He did, however, believe in *performing* apologies, although he wouldn't have framed it that way. When his mother-in-law became seriously ill and moved into an assisted-living residence a few miles from their home, Marvin stepped up and did an exceptional job on the caretaking scene. I witnessed in amazement as he proved to be, quite late in the game, a model husband and son-in-law. He told me he was going to try to set things right and make up for what he hadn't done in the past.

Without complaint, Marvin tirelessly helped his mother-in-law during the three-year period preceding her death, despite her being a difficult woman who never said thank you, and who had a conflicted relationship with Bernice. Marvin took his mother-in-law for medical treatments and stepped in whenever his wife felt overloaded. His mother-in-law was a religious person, though he and Bernice were not, and Marvin brought her to church every Sunday for as long as she was able to attend. When she died he made telephone calls and funeral arrangements, at his wife's request. Bernice and Marvin's marriage was strengthened and I believe they were happier together than ever before.

It's Not Just the Marvins in the World Who Perform Apologies

Even some very articulate, let's-talk-about-it type of folks may prefer not to bring up their less-than-honorable past behavior because they fear it may make things worse, or they don't want to face the longer conversation that will ensue.

A therapy client of mine left her teenage daughter

with a friend's family for her junior and senior years of high school, while she moved in with a new boyfriend halfway across the country. Much later she felt a deep regret, but it didn't feel right to open up a conversation about it. Even though she was a therapist herself, she couldn't bring herself to do it. Instead, when her daughter gave birth to twins, she relocated to be near her, and did a great deal of hands-on grandparenting. She told me it was her way of making up for the past and balancing the scales of justice.

Of course, language matters, and I am writing a book that argues for that. Without the language of "I'm sorry" and heartfelt words of remorse, there might always be the sense of something missing. Still, love and remorse can be communicated in different ways, and apologies take different forms.

Even the most entrenched non-apologizer may have a nonverbal way to try to defuse tension, reconnect after a fight, or show you through behavior that he or she is sorry and wants to make amends. Aim to make your default position one of generosity of spirit.

NOT EVERYTHING IS FORGIVABLE

Accepting an apology doesn't always mean reconciliation. The best apology in the world can't restore every connection. The words "I'm sorry" may be absurdly inadequate even if sincerely offered. Sometimes the foundation of trust on which a relationship was built cannot be repaired. We may never want to see the person who hurt us again.

We can still accept the apology.

All the King's Horses and All the King's Men

JoAnn called me for a brief consultation regarding her ex–best friend Marsha. They had been friends for seven years before Marsha took a job at the same firm where JoAnn worked. It was here that Marsha betrayed JoAnn's confidence, used her words against her, and sabotaged her chance at a promotion they both wanted. JoAnn ended up leaving the firm and their friendship ended for good.

The two women hadn't seen or spoken to each other for about four years when JoAnn received a long email from Marsha that contained a heartfelt apology in which she expressed regret and remorse for her earlier behavior. Marsha had done some soul-searching. She told JoAnn that she missed her terribly and wanted to renew the friendship. She asked JoAnn to email a few dates when they might meet for lunch to talk. She ended her email with, "I hope you'll forgive me."

"How do I respond?" was the question that JoAnn wanted my help with. She believed that Marsha's apology was sincere, but as she talked about the possibility of meeting for lunch it was clear that every cell in her body rebelled against getting together. JoAnn considered not responding at all, but ignoring Marsha's email violated JoAnn's own sense of integrity.

After considering her options, JoAnn sent this email:

> *Dear Marsha,*
> *Thank you for your note of apology. I'm glad that you've given so much thought to what happened between us and how your behavior affected me. For me, there is too much water under the bridge to talk further or to try to continue the friendship. I wish you well, and I, too, have many good memories from our long history together.*
>
> *Best,*
> *JoAnn*

I told JoAnn I thought it was an exemplary email. It was short (always best), cordial, and to the point. JoAnn didn't say, "I forgive you," because she didn't. She avoided rehashing Marsha's crime sheet or noting how Marsha's actions had devastated her. JoAnn didn't muddle the clarity of her communication by saying, "Perhaps with more time I'll feel differently," which would have left open the possibility of resuming a friendship that JoAnn didn't want.

Although JoAnn was initially tempted to say, "I can't accept your apology," she chose instead to thank Marsha for it. It was a sign of JoAnn's maturity that she wanted to keep her response congruent with her own values, and not just react in kind to how badly Marsha had behaved. "Thank you for the apology" did not mean the relationship could be restored to what it was before, or that JoAnn was up for even one more exchange. Not everything we break can be fixed.

THE COURAGE TO SAY
"I DON'T ACCEPT YOUR APOLOGY"

Sometimes we don't accept an apology for good reason. Perhaps the apologizer hasn't really listened, or just can't get it, or implies that it's our overreaction or misreading of things that's the real problem.

Or perhaps we're tired of hearing an apology or a passionate expression of remorse that's obviously empty because the person continues the very behavior that they are apologizing for, whether it's checking their phone during mealtime or failing to do the things that they've promised to do. If the person has not put a sincere effort into ensuring that there is no repeat performance, we're likely to let them know that we don't want to hear their repeated apologies.

When an apology sounds false or tries to reverse blame, it can take courage to call the person on it. I recall a memorable example of this when I was with a few parents who were talking in a school playground about the lack of diversity in the elementary school classrooms. One mother said that her son had two black kids in his class, with the tag line ". . . but they seem very clean and well behaved." One of the dads, a friend of mine, said calmly, "Black *but* clean and well-behaved? Help me understand what you mean here." The mother became very defensive, as any of us might when we are confronted with underlying racism.

The next day this mother saw my friend again in the playground and said, "I want to apologize. I'm really sorry that you heard my comment as racist because that's certainly not how I meant it." He said quietly, "If you see the problem as my reaction, and not what you said, I'm afraid I can't accept your apology." When she insisted that he was reading things into her comment that weren't there, and added she was fed up with walking on eggshells trying to be politically correct, he scratched his head and said, Columbo-style, "Well, I guess we see this one differently," and left it at that.

I admired him a lot for this one, especially as he didn't do her the favor of arguing with her or pressing the point. Instead, he left her the space to reckon with the implication of her own words. Perhaps at some point she'll be able to do that.

LEAN INTO GENEROSITY

As a general rule, consider keeping your default position as accepting the olive branch, even if privately you're unhappy with aspects of the apology. Of course there will be exceptions, but in general, it's simply not useful to get into a tug-of-war about apologies or to expect that the other person's apology will meet all the criteria of the effective apology that I outline in this book. Erring on the side of acceptance will create more possibilities for the future of the relationship.

Accepting an apology or peace offering does not necessarily mean that you are finished talking about a painful issue or that you forgive the other person for what they've said or done, or not said or done. It can be less a way of saying, "Okay, the past is past and there is no need to revisit it," and more a way of saying that there is still a future in which something other than anger and resentment is possible.

Accepting the olive branch simply means that you agree to end a fight, lower the intensity, and open a space for moving forward with goodwill. This will also pave the way for the possibility of more conversation on the very subject you may still be angry about. Of course, some apologies don't merit our acceptance, but in general it's best to accept an apology with a generous spirit and see where the relationship can go from there.

CHAPTER 8

Who Is at Fault?
When Reconciliation
Grinds to a Halt

It's in our most enduring and significant relationships that people become too mad to apologize. One or both parties may be convinced that the relationship can't move forward if the other doesn't consider his or her behavior and apologize for it. Yet there may be little agreement on who started it, what the offense is, what's required to mend it, and who needs to apologize first.

You can learn the "how-to's" of crafting an excellent apology, but that won't help you if you don't have the motivation to offer one. Under stress, people easily get polarized and divide into opposing camps. We get overfocused on what the other party is doing *to* us or not doing *for* us, and underfocused on our own creative options to move differently and de-intensify the situation. We want change but we don't want to change first—a great recipe for relationship failure.

What follows is a typical example of a married couple stuck in negativity and blame, where neither wants to apologize to the other, to say nothing of making the behavioral changes that would give their apology meaning. The lessons contained here are relevant for whatever significant relationships you're in, whether it's with a family member or a close friend. Relationships get in and out of trouble in predictable and patterned ways.

SHE SAYS/HE SAYS

Consider this typical angry exchange that took place in my consulting room between Ina and Sam, a couple in their forties who had been married for fifteen years:

SHE SAYS that she wants to discuss an incident that had occurred several days earlier in the Chicago airport. Sam brought the luggage out to the car where she was parked, and forgot her messenger bag, which contained her wallet, iPhone, important work papers, "my whole life." Sam retrieved it without incident but Ina's still angry, not only that he left something so valuable unattended by the baggage claim, but because he just didn't get how serious his inattentiveness was. "Rather than showing any kind of normal reaction," she tells me, "he curtly states he'll go back for it, as if it's no big deal." She goes on to say that when Sam showed up with her bag, he offered the obligatory apology and announced that he didn't want to hear any more about it, that the conversation was over. "This is not an isolated incident," she tells me. "Sam can't be counted on to follow through on things and pay attention. When I call him on something his standard response is, 'I don't want to talk about it.' He doesn't want to talk about anything. He just wants to be left alone to do his work."

HE SAYS that he's been schlepping all the luggage on this trip without complaint because Ina has a bad back. In fact, he says he's been doing a million things for her, but the focus is always on his deficiencies. "Everything is expected of me, and then it's all about what I don't do right." He adds that she always blows things out of proportion. It's not just that he forgot her messenger bag, but once again he's an irresponsible person who she can never count on. He turns to her and says wryly, "Mrs. Stark, my third-grade teacher, gave me a B-plus in *Attention* and *Good Citizenship*, but you give me a D-minus even though I do way more than my share." To me he says, "Ina will never let this thing go until I agree that I have some big problem here. And what are the chances that someone is going to steal a bag that's sitting next to the baggage claim? Was it really such a life-and-death emergency? Does everything have to be a crisis?"

Not Just a Bad Day

Some variation of this fight could take place in one form or another between even the most loving partners at a particularly stressful time. We all have varied levels of functioning that we may bring to family relationships. If you had been a fly on the wall during my very worst fights with Steve, you would probably shut this book immediately. Even happy couples can have some terrible fights and manage to patch them up with no lingering resentments.

In contrast, Ina and Sam were not having the occasional bad day or even a sustained rough period. Rather, their nonproductive fighting and criticism were eroding the foundation of love and friendship on which their relationship had been built. Like most couples they had started their marriage fully intending to be loving and generous partners, vowing to listen carefully to each other and repair any harm they had done. But now each felt like the "done-in" partner, and neither could let go of their insistence on being right.

Here were two highly intelligent people who would have no trouble learning the various components of the good apology. But an apology was the last thing that either was willing to offer the other.

Perhaps you can imagine ways that either Ina or Sam could have de-escalated their downward-spiraling interaction at the airport. Ina, for her part, could have toned down her criticism. She could have shared how terrified she felt at the possibility of losing her bag, without the accompanying anger and blame. Sam, for his part, could have offered an emotion-packed apology for his mistake: "Oh, my God, I can't believe I did that! Let me race back right now and get it for you. I am so sorry!" When he returned with the messenger bag, he might have jumped in to reinforce his apology, rather than waiting for the criticism he knew was coming: "Ina, I can't tell you how relieved I felt when I saw your bag was still there. I can't believe I left it there!"

Obviously, Sam's *under*reaction had something to do with Ina's *over*reaction, and vice versa. If Sam or Ina had been traveling with a friend or coworker instead of with each other, I'm sure they would each have responded more generously to the same messenger bag scenario. We all have a better self we can reach for, but sometimes our anger, fear, stress, or exhaustion blocks us from doing so.

It's a Circular Dance

The interaction at the airport is one snapshot of the larger portrait of Sam and Ina's marriage. Sam managed his emotional intensity by distancing and Ina managed hers by critical pursuit. Pursuing and distancing are patterned ways that humans move under stress to try to get comfortable. Neither is right or wrong, good or bad, but when a pursuer and distancer pair up, they can get locked into extreme positions.

Obviously, relationships go best when one or both parties have the flexibility to modify their style. But by the time I first saw Sam and Ina in therapy, the pattern was entrenched. While Sam's style of distancing made him appear like the cooler, more rational, and less difficult of the two, this was not the case. Distancing is simply one style of managing intense emotions. It's neither better nor worse than Ina's style of moving into the fray.

Who's to Blame?

Let's imagine two people observing Sam and Ina's marriage over time. The first observer might say: "The poor guy! He's married to such a controlling, critical bitch. Of course he distances. Who wouldn't want to get away from her? What else can he do? She never gets off his back. *She* should apologize first!"

"No," says observer number two. "You have it all wrong. Her husband has left her totally alone in this marriage. He doesn't let her legitimate complaints affect him. He shuts her out and doesn't care about her feelings. No wonder she's desperate. *He* should apologize first!"

We automatically look for the one to blame, the person who "started it," but relationships don't work that way. Both observers are right and both are wrong. Relationships operate in a circular, not linear, fashion, the behavior of each person provoking and reinforcing the behavior of the other. The real question is not who started it, or who is to blame, but rather what each person can do to change his or her steps in the dance.

"I'm Sorry for My Part" Is a Good First Step

Apologizing for our part is a good thing to do, when we know what our part is. It's not a real apology to

say, "I'm sorry for my part," if we have zero motivation to observe and change our contribution and we
think our behavior is necessary and justified because
we're giving that person what they need or deserve.
It would take courage for either Ina or Sam to offer
an apology for their part that reflects goodwill and
authentic claiming of responsibility. But an apology is
not enough. At least one of them needs to also change
his or her entrenched way of moving under stress.

While a simple apology can often repair specific
hurts and grievances, entrenched patterns like this
one need a different approach. While it's ideal for
two people to be working on changing their part in
a relationship problem, it's more common that only
one person (usually the person in more pain) has
his or her motor running for change. Happily, even
a slight modification by one person can make a big
difference, because once you change your steps the
old dance can't continue as usual. Here are some approaches that might work well for Sam and Ina, and
that would back an apology with a significant shift in
behavior.

MOVING AGAINST DISTANCE:
THE CHALLENGE FOR SAM

Sam had long ago given up on Ina, concluding he had
likely married the wrong person, even though her vitality, openness, and strong emotional expressiveness
were exactly what once drew him to her. If he really

wants to revive their relationship, he will need to find the courage to move toward Ina, to be creative in closing the distance between them in any way he can.

He might begin by offering a heartfelt apology: "Ina, I am so sorry that I haven't really listened to you and that I've so often refused to talk about things that matter to you. That was wrong and I'm working on changing that. I'm your partner and I want to be here to talk to you about anything."

Along with words of apology, Sam can move toward greater connection. He can make an effort to give Ina his attention and full presence. He might consult her about problems he faces at work or with his family and then value her input. When Sam needs space, he can take it in a way that won't trigger pursuit. It's one thing, for example, to return to the office after dinner when he's made a plan to do so, and another to announce halfway through the meal that he's heading back to work as soon as dinner is over. Sam can also make sure that he's as reachable for Ina by phone or text as he would be for a business client or close friend. He can do the little things that make her feel loved, valued, and chosen, things he did automatically during the courtship stage of their relationship.

Will Sam *feel* like doing these things? Of course not. But if the relationship matters to him, he can do them anyway. It may help Sam to keep in mind that his distance is actually encouraging pursuit, and that the very qualities that make Ina "impossible to talk to" may have a great deal to do with the fact that she feels she can't reach him. It was true that Ina tended to overtalk things in a rapid-fire way when she was anxious, which was much of the time. It was also true that Sam's distance and stonewalling only raised her anxiety further and intensified her rat-a-tat-tat style of expressing her worries and complaints.

Finding Voice

Sam also needs to find his voice to tell Ina how much intensity he can manage. If he can't clarify the limits of his tolerance, he won't be able to move toward more connection.

Sam might approach Ina at a calm time when they're getting along and say warmly: *"Ina, I want to learn to listen to you better. I think because of all the fighting my parents did when I was growing up, I'm allergic to conflict and intensity. When you start off with a list of criticisms or you share your worries in such an intense way, I feel flooded and I know I withdraw. I want to be available to listen to everything—including your criticisms. But I can't do that without your help."*

Sam can also focus on Ina's positive qualities, which are inextricably interwoven with what's driving him crazy. He might say, *"I know, Ina, that what I react to in a negative way is the other side of what I love about you—your energy and vitality, and how openly you address things. No one in my family was good at that."*

Sam can tell Ina the specific changes he needs from her to help him to listen better. He can ask Ina to try to approach him calmly and without blame, and bring up one issue and criticism at a time. He can tell her that he's happy to set up a meeting to hear her criticisms and concerns, but that he can't listen when he walks in the door, or during dinner, or when he's tired. He can also refuse to participate in conversations that are at his expense, telling her, *"Ina, I want to hear what you're saying, but I can't listen when you approach me like I'm a big screw-up. Come back when you can talk to me calmly and with respect."*

The courage and clarity to define our bottom line, which includes our needs and the limits of our tolerance, is at the heart of having both a relationship and a self. Doing so is ultimately an act of kindness and respect. Most pursuers would rather be confronted by a strong partner with a clear request for a behavioral change, than be met with silence. A firm constructive complaint lets your partner know that you care about making the relationship better and that you're willing to fight for it.

In sum, Sam's attempts to muzzle Ina can only make things worse. Ina needed him to be there for her, to really get her, and to care about her feelings. The phrase, *"I don't want to talk about it"*—when it goes beyond taking temporary distance and becomes a pervasive strategy—is the death knell of an intimate relationship. Instead of shutting down, Sam needs to tell Ina, "I am always here to talk to you about anything that matters. But you need to help me out here, and here's how you can do it."

STOPPING THE PURSUIT: INA'S CHALLENGE

Ina, for her part, needs to dial down the criticism and make sure positive comments exceed negative ones by a healthy margin. As often happens in marriage, Ina had long ago stopped paying attention to what she liked and valued about Sam, and only commented on what she didn't like. Many of her criticisms were valid, but no one—whether nine or ninety—will value criticism if there is not a surrounding climate of appreciation and respect. Psychologist Ellen Wachtel states it simply: "We love those who make us feel good about ourselves." Where Sam is expecting criticism, Ina can surprise him with praise.

Getting out of pursuit mode with Sam requires Ina to do more than dialing down the criticism. It also means ratcheting down the intensity level by reducing or eliminating loud, fast-paced speech, interruption, overtalking, and offering advice or little corrections that aren't requested.

I'm not suggesting that these are neurotic traits or that Ina has some kind of personality disorder. A different partner than Sam might enjoy these very same qualities and consider himself lucky to have found such an articulate, impassioned, energetic partner. But Sam was viscerally allergic to intensity, and more so over time. Like many distancers, he'd say, "I don't like to talk," but he actually feared getting trapped in a conversation that felt awful to him.

Even positive intensity can lead to more distance

once the pursuit-distance dynamic is firmly in place. Being intensely generous or solicitous (frequently asking if your partner is okay, showering him or her with praise, wanting a "real kiss" while your partner is cooking dinner rather than a peck on the cheek) is unhelpful when a distancer is feeling crowded. Lowering intensity doesn't just mean shifting it from negative to positive. With a partner like Sam, it means dialing it all down, at least for a while, to observe the results of your own experiment.

Ina also had the challenge of not taking Sam's need for space quite so personally. His cool, self-sufficient style was part of what initially attracted Ina to him, but what initially attracts us is often what later drives us crazy. Sam was a private person who didn't want to debrief after every dinner party or talk in detail about the symptoms of his stomach flu. He shut down more when pushed to share his thoughts and feelings. Like many men he came to couples counseling with Ina's footprint on the seat of his pants. He was generally a do-it-yourselfer who calmed himself by seeking space when he was stressed. When we interpret genuine difference as a problematic distance, we end up making things worse.

Accepting differences is one of the greatest of all human challenges, and that includes differences in how we manage stress. One of my favorite cartoons by my friend the humorist Jennifer Berman shows a dog and cat in bed together. The dog is looking morose and reading a book called *Dogs Who Love Too Much*. The cat is saying, "I'm not distancing! I'm a cat, damn it." I love this cartoon, because it highlights how couples can get in trouble when they can't appreciate or at least accept differences. Maintaining privacy wasn't just Sam's way of hiding out, but also his preferred way of being in the world. Ina will do better if she can accept and even welcome his way rather than wasting energy trying to change it. Under stress Sam will naturally seek more separateness, just as Ina will naturally seek more togetherness.

Ina can also break the pursuit cycle by focusing less on Sam, and instead put her primary energy into ensuring the quality and direction of her own life. She might offer the following words of apology: "Sam, I'm truly sorry that I've been on your back so much. I realize that I need to pay more attention to things I'm neglecting in my own life, like how distant I am from my brother right now, and what I need to do next since I've left my job as a paralegal. I've been noticing how often I get critical of you when I'm not feeling good about myself. I'm going to get a grip on that."

It's almost always useful to apologize to the person we've been *over*focused on in a worried or blaming way, and explain that we've been *under*focused on our own self. Becoming more self-focused helps loosen up the pursuer-distancer dynamic, and puts us on firmer footing, no matter how the other person responds.

Change Is a Long-Term Project

While Sam and Ina had very different styles of navigating their relationship under stress, they essentially faced the same challenge:

* *To offer an apology when an apology is due.*

* *To make the other feel special, valued, and chosen.*

* *To respect differences, including different ways of responding to stress.*

* *To focus on changing their own steps in the dance rather than waiting for the other to change first.*

* *To stop the negative comments that erode the foundation of marriage and friendship, and replace them with positive ones.*

These are good guidelines to follow in any relationship. The challenge is often greatest for couples and family members because these relationships act like a lightning rod that absorbs stress from every source.

SHOULD YOU FAKE IT?

A familiar joke among men maintains that the husband should always have the last word in any confrontation—

and that last word should be, "You're right, honey. I'm wrong. I'm sorry and I'll never do it again."

The meaning of the joke is clear. Women are so difficult to engage with that it's best for the poor husband to apologize just to keep the peace. It's insulting to the woman because it suggests that she's so unreasonable that it's impossible to deal with her directly. It's insulting to the man as well, because it assumes he can't find his voice, or maybe he never had one to begin with. The backstory of the joke is that the purpose of an apology to a female partner is to escape a longer, unwanted conversation.

In contrast, we can choose to offer an apology—even when we think the disagreement is mostly not our fault—with a courageous intention. We may know that a real conversation will not take place until at least one person calms down, and so we may offer the olive branch to create a calmer emotional climate in which two people can begin to hear each other, or at least stay in the same room. We may say, "I'm sorry for my part in this," without yet being clear about our contribution, but with goodwill and a commitment to think about it. Here our goal is to widen the path for intimacy over time, not to settle for a superficial and premature peace.

Creative Pretending Can Save Your Relationship

When you're in the emotional soup, like Sam and Ina, it may feel impossible to warm things up and apologize first. Any sort of "be positive" advice of the sort I gave each of them may make you want to gag because it doesn't feel real. But here's the paradox: Sometimes we can only learn what is real or possible by restraining our so-called "true self" and engaging in creative pretending. In contrast to the "I'm sorry" in the apology joke, creative pretending is motivated by courage and a spirit of adventure—not by fear or the wish to avoid conflict at all costs.

Words like *pretending* have decidedly negative connotations for women, and for good reason. Many of us were encouraged to deny legitimate anger and protest, to please and protect men at the expense of the self, and to hold relationships in place as if our lives depended on it. We were taught to apologize for using up valuable oxygen in the room, and to wrap guilt and self-doubt around ourselves like an old familiar blanket.

No one aspires to be phony, or to hang out in a relationship where they can't be real. Intimacy in family and friendship requires that we can deepen and refine the truths we tell each other, and that we can bring our full selves into the relationship. Yet there is nothing honest about a life lived on automatic pilot where doing what comes naturally will naturally go nowhere or make things worse. Indeed, changing how we habitually behave in any relationship often requires an initial willingness to pretend, to do something different that may at first feel nothing like being one's true self.

An old Spanish proverb reminds us that habits are first silken threads and then become cables. Change

is not easy, including for those who are actively pushing for it. Yet we are capable of surprising changes
when we can no longer live with the status quo. The
distancer can make a forceful effort to connect, to ask
questions and listen with the intention to understand.
The overtalker can practice brevity and leaving more
space. The fix-it person can dial down the advice-
giving, little corrections, and "I know-what's-best" attitude. The rigid partner can learn to bend like grass,
and the overly accommodating partner can learn to
stand like an oak when something really matters.

I could make a longer list, but you get the idea. You
need to be yourself and also to "try out a new you."
Without a spirit of adventure, you'll be stuck with a
narrow vision of who you are and what's possible in
your relationships. The best apologies are offered by
people who understand that it is important to be oneself, but equally as important to choose the self that
we want to be.

IT'S A LONG-DISTANCE RUN

We can apologize to someone in thirty seconds,
but changing our part in a relationship impasse is a
long-distance run that takes endurance, and the capacity to push forward in the face of enormous resistance
from within and without. At the same time, the process
requires restraint. It asks us to sit still when we feel
fired up to speak and act, and to have the wisdom and
intuition to know how and when to say what to whom.

Changing an entrenched pattern also requires patience. Obviously, Ina couldn't modulate her intensity overnight, any more than Sam could stay calm and present when she flew into pursuit mode. The substantive changes that give an apology its meaning may occur slowly. It's the direction, not the speed, of travel that matters.

CHAPTER 9

The Most Stunning Apology I Ever Witnessed

C ertain apologies are so courageous that the very word *apology* seems too glib. Letty's story, for example, falls on the heroic end of the apology spectrum.

LETTY AND KIM

I had been Letty's therapist for some time when I suggested that she invite her twenty-four-year-old daughter Kim to join us for a session. What was happening was this: Kim had been avoiding her, and something was obviously wrong. But when Letty inquired, Kim snapped, "I don't want to talk about it."

When Kim was twelve, her father had entered her bedroom when he thought she was sleeping and molested her. Letty was out of town moving her own mother into an assisted living place, and didn't know for several months that this had happened. When the facts came out in the open, Letty responded appropriately by getting the whole family into treatment. They were fortunate to see an excellent therapist who was helpful to them.

Letty considered the issue resolved, but trauma is never fully resolved, certainly not as if it had never occurred in the first place. Kim's dad had recently died of a heart attack, and I suspected his death had stirred everything up again, including Kim's enormous rage.

Kim first refused Letty's invitation to join us, but a few months later she agreed to come just once. When I asked Kim how she had been doing since her father's death, she launched into a terrible attack on Letty. Although I'm trained to be a calm presence in an intense emotional field, my own anxiety rose in response to the raw rage that Kim directed not at her deceased father, but instead toward her mother. It felt as if Kim blamed Letty for her father's behavior, and was locating the betrayal in the family between mother and daughter, which is not unusual for daughters to do.

I was about to intervene when Letty rose from her chair and pulled it closer to Kim's. I thought she was going to yell back at her daughter something like, "How dare you say this to me! How can you blame me for what your father did? How could I have known?"

Instead, Letty turned to her daughter in the most fully present way and said: "I'm so sorry, Kim. I'm so sorry I didn't know. I'm so sorry I didn't protect you. I'm so sorry that this terrible thing happened in our family. I'm so sorry that you didn't feel safe enough to tell me the truth." Then Letty started to cry. Kim put her arms around her mother, and they cried together.

I don't know how Letty was able to be there for her daughter in such a remarkably open and nondefensive way. Letty didn't say she was sorry because she believed the abuse had been her fault or because she thought that she had been a bad mother. But now, in the face of being totally blasted, she moved into a place of pure listening and offered her love.

Letty's tears did not serve to silence her daughter's anger or to make her own pain the focus of the conversation. Nor was she inviting Kim to comfort or protect her. Her apology for being part of this wrenching history was heartfelt and deeply healing for her and her daughter.

Letty's apology was especially healing because it didn't include any add-ons. She didn't say, "I'm sorry, but you need to keep in mind I didn't know it was happening." Or, "I'm sorry, but your dad was a weak man, and I don't think he could help himself." Or, "I'm sorry, but this happened a long time ago, and I wish we could put this behind us and move on." She didn't even say, "I'm sorry and I hope you'll forgive me." Of course, Letty hoped Kim would forgive her. But a true apology does not ask the other person to do anything—not even to forgive.

"I'm Sorry" Is Just the First Step

Letty deserved a badge of honor for the pure apology that she offered Kim, and when I saw her the following week she understandably wished that it would put closure on the pain of the past. We all might wish that even the most emotionally painful issues could be resolved in one conversation, but it doesn't work that way.

I learned in a subsequent therapy session that there had been no conversation about the sexual abuse after the family therapy terminated when Kim was thirteen. Letty's silence over all the years after the therapy ended was her loving way of protecting her daughter. But in Letty's desire to avoid being intrusive or making things worse, she unwittingly left her daughter unutterably alone with the worst thing that had ever happened to her. When people suffer, as Kim did, they often suffer twice, first because they have lived through something painful, and second because a key person in their lives doesn't want to hear about it, or doesn't want to hear all of it.

A few therapy sessions later, Letty told me about a Saturday night movie and dinner date that she had initiated with her daughter a week following the funeral service for Kim's dad. Letty chose the film they saw together, not knowing that it contained a scene in which a teenage girl was raped by a hired hand. When the two women grabbed a bite to eat afterward and did their usual "postmortem" of the movie, neither mentioned the sexual violence.

"Did the rape scene in the movie remind you of what happened to Kim in your family?" I inquired.

"Of course it went through my mind," Letty replied. "And I'm sure Kim thought of it, too. How could she not? She was in a foul mood when we left the theater, and my choice of the movie probably contributed to it."

"Did you consider saying something about it?" I asked. It was, after all, on both of their minds.

"No," said Letty. "My plan was to have a fun evening, and it was my mistake to pick this movie to begin with. I wasn't going to make things worse by bringing up the sexual abuse. It's Kim's place to mention it, if she wants to talk about it."

The rape scene in the movie was an obvious trigger for both of them. Given the prominence of sexual abuse in media, it was undoubtedly one of countless reminders of what happened to Kim. This movie, however, was the first trigger that followed the death of Kim's dad, and that preceded Kim's distancing from Letty.

What if Letty had done something different after leaving the movie? Imagine that Letty had turned to Kim and, with the same openheartedness that she showed in her apology, said something like this:

> *"Kim, I'm so sorry that I chose this movie for us, because I wanted this to be a fun time for us. I don't want to make the evening heavy, so I'm hesitant to say anything at all. I just want you to know that as I watched that rape scene I could only think of what your dad did to you, and it was painful to watch. I want you to know that I love you, and you're not alone with the pain of what happened."*

How might Kim have responded? Surely anxiety would rise like steam. Kim would likely have said something curt like, "I don't want to talk about it." Or, "Forget it. Don't worry about it." Nor is late Saturday night the best time to discuss a heavy issue that hasn't been mentioned since she was thirteen years old. It wouldn't be easy to continue this conversation in even the most optimal of circumstances.

But what about Kim's *long-term* response? I imagine, as her mother's words settled in over time, Kim might have felt something akin to a sense of gratitude that her mother had reached out to her in this way.

Continuing the Conversation

When I asked Letty to consider where the conversation might go following her powerful apology to Kim in the therapy session, she gave the predictable response. "I'll wait to see if Kim brings anything up," she said, "I want to follow her lead on this." With the best of intentions we almost always leave it to the hurt party to reopen the conversation about a painful or traumatic past event. But it shouldn't just be the hurt party's job. It becomes their job because they are so often left with it.

As we talked more, Letty began to recognize that it was important to say something to Kim that recognized the importance of the previous therapy session that included her. Total silence would be a form of distancing. At the very least, it would be a lost opportunity.

So after Letty left my office she steeled herself, took some deep breaths, and made herself call Kim. She thanked Kim for joining her in the therapy session, and added, "I've been thinking about how I never asked you any questions over all those years about how you were doing with the sexual abuse, how it was affecting you growing up, and what kind of leftover anxiety or anger you still have. It really hit me during the movie we saw after Dad died, but I couldn't bring myself to say anything at dinner."

"It doesn't matter," Kim said flatly. "I didn't want to talk about it."

"It matters to me. I want to have a relationship with you where we can talk about what's important."

"I don't see the point," Kim said.

"I hope we can talk later," Letty said.

No one wants to be intrusive or dredge up the past when the other person wants to put it to rest. The past, however, was already dredged up. I encouraged Letty to take the initiative to keep the conversation going, using her own good sense of timing and intuition. The challenge was to keep the lines of communication open to allow for conversation as it might arise over time, without getting overfocused on the sexual abuse, or trying to do too much too fast.

One Thing Leads to Another

It was a bit of a tightrope walk, but Letty did her best to maintain her balance. She didn't pressure Kim to talk, but neither did she return to her previous silence. Letty found ways to test the waters. She began by asking Kim a few factual (rather than emotionally loaded) questions when the opportunity arose, like, "Does your best friend Linda know about the sexual abuse?" "How did Linda respond?" "Is there anyone else that you trusted enough to tell?"

Letty also returned to her own contribution to the painful history, the part she now looked back on with sincere regret. She said, "Kim, since your dad died, I've been thinking about the fact that I never asked you one question about the sexual abuse after we stopped the family therapy. Even when it was on my mind, I didn't talk to you about it. I didn't bring it up because I thought if you weren't bringing it up, I shouldn't bring it up. That was a mistake. I left you alone with it. I'm so sorry."

"You don't need to apologize again," said Kim. "Enough already."

"Okay, I won't apologize again. I just want you to know that when and if you feel ready to talk, I'm here to listen."

Because one thing leads to another, a couple of painful conversations took place several months later that left Letty feeling temporarily flattened and misunderstood. Most excruciating for Letty was when Kim confronted her about her marriage.

"So you stayed with Dad after knowing what he did to me," Kim said angrily one afternoon at lunch. "And you divorced him when I was seventeen because he had an affair? So his affair was a bigger deal to you than his molesting your daughter? Is that fucked up or what?"

Letty felt unable to speak, like the words were knocked out of her mouth. "It was like you never gave the abuse a second thought," Kim rushed on. "It's like you and Dad just put it behind you. I couldn't put it behind me. It happened to me."

This conversation would never have occurred if Letty had not opened the lines of communication. And who among us wouldn't prefer to avoid further accusations—which is why we so often don't take the conversation far enough to evoke the possibility of being slammed. Without the confidence to know that we can handle whatever comes next, and enough self-esteem to avoid collapsing into shame, it's unlikely that we will deepen the conversation.

Letty hung in even when she was suffering. She talked honestly with her daughter, explaining that her outrage about the affair, and her refusal to go to couples therapy before filing for divorce, was related to the sexual abuse. The affair precipitated the divorce, Letty said, because it reactivated her rage about the harm he had done to Kim. She told Kim that she never put the abuse behind her, not for a day. She revealed to Kim that she and Kim's father never resumed sexual relations, and that thoughts of leaving the marriage were always with her.

Letty told Kim that she didn't want to make excuses for her choices, and that she couldn't fully explain or justify her decisions, not even to herself. She could only tell Kim with 100 percent conviction that she would never, not for one second, compare a marital infidelity to the sexual violation that Kim experienced as a child.

"There are no words to tell you how sorry I am that I left you alone with what happened," Letty said. "I wish I could go back in time and do it differently. Is there any way that I can make it up to you?"

"You can't make it up to me," Kim said. Then she softened and added, "But at least I have my mother back."

CHAPTER 10

"You Need to Forgive" and Other Lies That Hurt You

A colleague and I have been discussing *Citizen* by Claudia Rankine, an African-American poet whose book captures the black experience of racism in white America, and, in this excerpt, an encounter with a white therapist:

> *The new therapist specializes in trauma counseling. You have only ever spoken to her on the phone. Her house has a side gate that leads to a back entrance she uses for patients. You walk down a path bordered on both sides with deer grass and rosemary to the gate, which turns out to be locked.*
>
> *At the front door the bell is a small round disc that you press firmly. When the door finally opens, the woman standing there yells, at the top of her lungs, Get away from my house! What are you doing in my yard?*

It's as if a wounded Doberman pinscher or a German shepherd has gained the power of speech. And though you back up a few steps, you manage to tell her you have an appointment. You have an appointment? she spits back. Then she pauses. Everything pauses. Oh, she says, followed by, oh, yes, that's right. I am sorry.

I am so sorry, so, so sorry.

It's a deeply powerful piece of writing. The words, "I am so sorry, so, so sorry," are absurdly inadequate even if sincerely felt. There is no way this therapist can make things right. The foundation of trust on which a relationship might have been built has collapsed beyond repair.

"I imagine it will be difficult for the speaker in this poem to ever forgive the therapist," my colleague comments. Our conversation has turned from the ongoing presence of racism to the subject of forgiveness.

"Why should she forgive?" I ask.

"She needs to forgive," he explains, "because there can be no peace or healing without forgiveness." He pauses, then adds, "I think one of the most challenging parts of my job is helping my clients learn to forgive—not to forget, but to forgive, even if they decide to never see the wrongdoer again."

My colleague goes on to describe the act of forgiveness as the greatest of virtues, the highest form of love, and a necessity for good mental and physical health. He quotes something I had seen on Facebook earlier that day: "To forgive is to set a prisoner free and to discover that the prisoner was you." Only forgiveness, he says, can free the injured party from holding on to their anger and hatred.

I disagree with these well-intentioned but potentially hurtful ideas; the idea that forgiveness is the *only* path to a life that's not mired down in bitterness and hate, and that those who do *not* forgive the unapologetic offender are less spiritually evolved persons at greater risk for emotional and physical problems. Contrast those ideas to the work of psychologist Janis Abrahms Spring, whose books provide an excellent counterpoint to the blanket cultural messages and clichés about the virtue and necessity of forgiving. Forgiveness, Spring says, is not a cheap gift. She notes that rushing to a premature and superficial peace can have its own costs.

I know, however, that the ideas my colleague put forth are commonly held by forgiveness experts, religious leaders, and popular culture as well. Yet there is little clarity in the literature about what "forgiveness" actually means. My own investigations into the subject suggest that no one definition fits all. More importantly, there are many paths to healing that do not require forgiveness. Let's begin then with defining our terms, or at least unpacking them.

WHAT DOES IT MEAN TO FORGIVE?

Many men and women come to therapy seeking relief from unrepaired hurts from the recent and far past.

The person who has hurt them has not earned forgiveness, whether through the simple act of saying, "I was wrong. I'm sorry," or through a longer process like that of Letty and Kim.

A comment like, "I want to forgive my father," may appear to be a simple statement, but it won't have the same meaning for everyone. For this reason I ask many questions that will help me to understand the meaning of this word for the particular individual who is seeking my help.

When I continue the conversation long enough, and listen carefully enough, I frequently learn that many men and women are not actually talking about forgiveness, although they may use that word. Instead they are talking about their desire to rid themselves of anger, bitterness, resentment, and pain. They want to feel like "a good person" and not like a spiteful, vengeful individual who sits around wishing that their best friend who violated an important confidence, or gossiped behind their back, would suffer some terrible misfortune. "I want to forgive" translates to, "I want to get past this and find some peace of mind."

Other individuals do seek to forgive the nonrepentant wrongdoer in the most profound spiritual sense of the word. Forgiveness may be a key part of their religious beliefs or central to their worldview. But many people just want the burden of their anger and resentment to go away. Words or phrases like *resolution*, *detachment*, *moving on*, or *letting go* may better describe what they seek.

A HEAVY LOAD: A ZEN TALE OF LETTING GO

There is a classic Zen story of letting go that is told in many different versions. Here's one retelling of this age-old Zen tale:

> *Two traveling monks came to a riverbank where a woman dressed in a long, silken dress rudely demanded to be carried over the swift water. The younger monk walked right by and proceeded to wade across the river. The older monk put the woman on his shoulders and carried her across. Upon reaching the other side, the arrogant woman strolled off without a kind word or even a simple expression of gratitude. Her attitude was clearly one of entitlement and contempt.*
>
> *As they continued on their way, it was clear that the young monk was becoming increasingly agitated and preoccupied. As they approached their destination many hours later, he was unable to stay silent.*
>
> *"How could you carry that woman?" he asked in a scolding tone. "You know that our vows prohibit us to touch a woman. Furthermore, she was spoiled and rude. She didn't even say thank you!"*
>
> *"I put the woman down when we crossed the river," the older monk replied. "Why are you still carrying her?"*

Letting go, as the older monk did, doesn't mean forgiving, forgetting, or whitewashing the other person's bad behavior. From a Buddhist perspective, the essence of forgiveness is letting go. But it by no means follows that you need to forgive a particular action in order to let go. I doubt if "forgiveness" entered the older monk's mind. He simply didn't take the woman's rudeness personally, didn't get hooked by or ruminative about it, and didn't wish her ill or need her to be different.

Letting go means protecting ourselves from the corrosive effects of staying stuck. Chronic anger and bitterness dissipate our energy and sap our creativity, to say nothing of ruining an otherwise good day. If nonproductive anger keeps us stuck in the past, we can't fully inhabit the present, nor can we move forward into the future with our full potential for optimism and joy. There is a difference between healthy anger that preserves the dignity and integrity of the self, and ruminative anger that wakes us up at three in the morning to nurse past and present grievances and drum up fantasies of revenge. The latter accomplishes nothing except to make us unhappy.

Needless to say, real-life situations that cause us suffering are not as simple as the Zen story of the two monks. It's easier to let go of rudeness from a stranger than to move on from the inexplicably hurtful actions of someone we have trusted and relied upon. Yet whether we have experienced a small hurt or a big betrayal, we don't need to forgive the actions of an unapologetic offender to find peace of mind. We do need, over time, to dissipate its emotional charge. We need to accept the reality that sometimes the wrongdoer is unreachable and unrepentant—or perhaps long dead—and we have a choice as to whether we continue to carry the wrongdoing on our shoulders or not.

Letting go is certainly not easy, but forgiveness need not be a part of that process when the wrongdoer has done nothing to earn it. There is no one path to healing.

NO ONE DEFINITION OF FORGIVENESS FITS ALL

The other day I happened upon these words from one of my favorite authors, Anne Lamott: "One of the most important gifts of spiritual faith is forgiveness, and I have grudgingly tugged this gift open over many years, and many hurts, until empathy for the other person has become almost a reflex." It's a lovely quote and I resonate totally with the essence of her message. But empathy isn't forgiveness and doesn't require forgiveness.

The conflating of *letting go* with *forgiving* confounds much of what's written about the necessity to forgive. If you read the research findings stating that nonforgiveness is bad for your well-being, the research might more accurately state that chronic, nonproductive anger and bitterness is bad for your health. Or that compassion and empathy, even for those who hurt us, are good things to cultivate. It's hard to argue with that. It's simply that none of these good things require forgiveness.

What Does Forgiveness Mean to You?

I have asked over a hundred people to define the word *forgiveness* as they experience it. Among the questions I asked were: "How do you know when you have forgiven someone? What are the signals and signs that tell you that you have fully forgiven someone, or that you are in the process of doing so?" I ask for specific examples. When it comes to forgiveness, we all use language differently while assuming that we're talking about the same thing.

What I've learned from these interviews confirms what I've observed in my clinical practice. Many people use the word for an experience of letting go of a hurt over time. They've stopped obsessing about the injury, and when they recall the hurtful behavior of the offender it has no emotional charge. When they talk about forgiving they are saying that when they think of the past offense it no longer bothers them. Or that sometimes the anger surfaces, but with decreasing frequency and intensity, and they have more distance from it.

Other people hold the word *forgiveness* to a high spiritual standard. "When I forgive, I surround the wrongdoer with love and light. I carry loving kindness in my heart for that person and wish them happiness and well-being." I have worked with people who possess a special capacity for forgiving the unforgivable, who teach and practice radical forgiveness—a form of love and compassion that is possible even for the most heinous acts and the most horrific of situations.

Forgiveness, from this latter perspective, does not just involve letting go for the sake of the hurt party. It goes further, recognizing the pain of the wrongdoer and wishing that he or she be happy and well. Not everyone is capable of radical forgiveness, nor does everyone strive for it. There is nothing lesser or closed-hearted about the person who seeks alternative strategies to releasing themselves from life-draining anger, bitterness, and pain.

What Forgiveness Means to Me

I use the word *forgiveness* sparingly and only when it is earned through a process of openhearted listening and self-examination. In the absence of a sincere apology—or some way a person might show me they are truly sorry and will not repeat the injury—I have no idea what it means to forgive a harmful or hurtful incident, though I know what it means to love that person anyway and wish them well.

For me, the word *forgive* is much like the word *respect*. It can't be commanded or demanded or forced, or gifted for no reason at all. When it comes to our close relationships, I agree with the words of Janis Abrahms Spring: "You don't restore your humanity when you forgive an unapologetic offender; he restores his humanity when he works to earn your forgiveness."

It's not that I identify with the label of an "unforgiving person." To the contrary, I know full well the first-hand experience of coming to a place of empathy and understanding for the very person who has injured me and never apologized for a particular action, never faced up to her insensitive or low-integrity behavior. My professional and life experiences have taught me to hold a large picture of people who do bad things, and I do not reduce them to their worst deeds or most dramatic insensitivities. I look at relationship problems, including my own, through the widest possible lens, and I teach people to understand patterns, rather than to blame or diagnose individuals.

That said, the word *forgiveness* is not a word I use to describe this compassionate or accepting place that I may or may not come to when I feel wronged by someone who can't get it, who is too defensive to take in what I am saying, and who will never genuinely feel that they have something to apologize for.

A Conversation with Ben

The complexity of this word *forgiveness* reminds me of a conversation I had with my younger son, Ben, when I was writing *The Mother Dance*. Ben, then a junior in high school, was taking issue with the title I had given to a particular chapter: "What Kind of Mother Ever Hates Her Children?" Ben argued that I should delete the word *hate* from my writing, that mothers don't hate their children. He was always up for a good debate.

As our conversation continued, it struck me that perhaps Ben was concerned that hate could permanently win out over love, that hate is fixed, while I argued that we can hate someone for thirty seconds, that there is nothing fixed in matters of the mind and heart, and that love and hate can coexist.

Somewhere, the conversation took a sudden turn.

"Would you love me if I murdered someone?" Ben challenged me. It was a typical Ben question.

I paused and he upped the ante. "What if I murdered Matt? Or Matt *and* Dad? Would you still love me?"

I told him I couldn't even wrap my brain around the question.

"If you did those things, you wouldn't be *you*," I said, but Ben kept pushing me for a response. Would I still love him?

My answer was *yes*. Yes, I would still love him.

His questions continued.

Yes, I would love him. Yes, I would visit him in jail. Yes, I would feel guilty and crazed. Yes, I would hate him. No, I would not lie for him. No, I would not forgive him. Yes, I would love him, he would always be a part of me.

Ben was satisfied.

I was glad that Ben could embrace the complexity. I couldn't imagine forgiving him, nor would I cast him out of my life. I would not cease to both love and hate him. When forgiveness experts talk in binary language ("You either forgive the wrongdoer or you are a prisoner of your own anger and hate"), they are collapsing the messy complexity of human emotions into a simplistic dichotomous equation. Even when my two boys were young they knew better than that.

"CAN'T YOU FORGIVE HIM?"
THE VERY WORDS THAT DON'T HELP

If you believe that forgiveness, like gratitude, is a universally healing emotion, you may be inclined to encourage other people to forgive someone who hurt them. Your intentions may be good, but you run the risk of victimizing the hurt party all over again.

Think back to the healing process between Letty and her daughter Kim in the last chapter. When Kim said to Letty, ". . . at least I have my mother back," she was coming from a place of genuine forgiveness. Letty had earned Kim's forgiveness through wholehearted listening, by validating Kim's experience over time, by taking the initiative to keep the difficult conversation going, and by offering a clear and unequivocal apology for the specific ways she had let Kim down.

Consider how differently their relationship would have gone if Letty had responded to Kim's anger by saying, "Kim, what your dad did happened a very long time ago. I made mistakes, too, but we all do. I don't see how it can help to keep digging up the past and holding on to old resentments. Can't you just forgive and move on?"

Such words, even if spoken with the best of intentions, would have left Kim feeling alone and abandoned all over again. She would likely have held on even tighter to her anger, which would have continued to run like a quiet river of pain underneath all of Kim's interactions with her mother. All credit goes to Kim's mother for never asking her daughter to forgive.

What *does* the hurt party need to hear? People who appear to be holding on to anger or bitterness frequently did not experience a clear, direct, heartfelt validation soon after an earlier betrayal or act of neglect occurred. The child, or adult, may have been told that the bad thing was not really happening, that his feelings and perceptions were wrong, out of proportion, or crazy—or that what happened was necessary, even his fault, his choice, and something he brought on by his own difficult behavior.

To heal, the hurt party needs to hear an unequivocal validation of the awfulness of the experience, and an affirmation that his or her feelings and perception make sense. Suggesting to someone that they forgive can leave the hurt party feeling more emotionally unsteady and betrayed all over again. This can be so, even if the injury and insults were small ones, and especially if they were not.

"Can't you forgive him?" are the last words a hurt or victimized person needs to hear. Clichés like, "She did the best she could," or "It is what it is," or "This happened forty years ago," are similarly unhelpful. It is one thing to tell someone that you hope they can find a way to unburden themselves from carrying so much anger and pain. It is another thing entirely to suggest that they should absolve the wrongdoer and transcend their anger through a heroic act of will or grace.

A LITTLE BIT FORGIVEN

Forgiveness is often characterized as an all-or-nothing sort of thing, like being pregnant. Either you embrace or exile the offender, either you forgive him or you don't. The truth is that you can forgive the other person 95 percent or 2 percent or anywhere in between. My therapy clients often feel surprised and relieved when I share this simple idea. The message resonates. The following example illustrates the point.

Should I Forgive Him for the Affair?

Rosa and her husband, Sam, came to see me in therapy after Rosa discovered that Sam was having an affair. Sam did not deny his infidelity and when she forcefully confronted him, he immediately ended all contact with the affair partner.

I was glad that Rosa didn't automatically make this a deal-breaker. An affair is not a terrible aberration that occurs only in unhappy marriages. Affairs can happen in excellent marriages as well. Theirs had been a good relationship with a long history, and they had two sons, ages seven and ten. Perhaps his eagerness to join her in couples therapy was the first step in leaving room for the possibility of forgiveness.

Reweaving the fabric of their marriage would be slow and arduous work. Rosa was understandably devastated that the man she counted on to be faithful had been lying to her for almost a year—the many layers of deception adding unspeakable pain to the sexual betrayal. Sam's countless apologies and expressions of remorse did not keep Rosa from feeling periodically enraged, depressed, crazy, disoriented, obsessed with the details of the affair, and convinced that nothing in her life would ever be normal again. Her anger and pain did not magically disappear in response to Sam's sincere, repeated efforts to demonstrate that he was now committed to truth telling, to avoiding future temptations, and to doing whatever it took to make amends.

Rosa would feel okay, but then, without warning, something would again trigger the full emotional weight of Sam's betrayal. Over and over she needed to talk about it. Sam became a brilliant listener. With the help of my coaching and Janis Abrahms Spring's book *After the Affair*, which I asked him to read, Sam became committed to hearing her rage and sorrow for as long as it took, which sometimes seemed to him like forever.

Sam was gradually able to take in Rosa's pain and carry it, as Letty did with her daughter Kim. Instead of waiting in dread for Rosa to bring up the affair for what felt to him like the millionth time, Sam learned to *initiate* the conversations himself. He checked in with Rosa on how she was doing, and let her know that he was continuing to think about how terribly he had hurt her. He did not leave her alone with her pain, or with the responsibility to keep the conversation going.

Spring calls this "the transfer of vigilance." In affairs, she explains, the unfaithful partner may complain that his partner remains obsessed with the betrayal despite his repeated apologies. He understandably wants her to move on. But Spring points out that if he's not available to hear her pain, take it in, hold it, and pay attention to it, she won't heal. Her book was a crucial resource for Sam during the long bumpy process of restoring trust. "I'm sorry, please forgive me," isn't going to cut it, even if repeated one thousand times.

Several years after Rosa and Sam terminated therapy, they called to request one more session to consult about a parenting dilemma with their older son. At the end of the hour, Sam turned to Rosa and, suddenly changing the topic, he asked her whether she had forgiven him. It was obviously a question he had asked Rosa many times before, but now it seemed out of the blue. I imagine our meeting together was a sharp reminder of what had brought them to my consulting room to begin with.

Rosa was silent for a long moment. She appeared to be uncertain as to how to respond. She then recalled a comment I had made when we terminated our earlier work together—that she could forgive whatever percentage she chose, or not at all, and that she did not need to give away all her anger to continue in the marriage, and feel love and compassion for Sam.

"Ninety percent," she announced. Sam looked at her quizzically.

"I forgive you for having the affair," she said, in a

voice that conveyed considerable assurance. "But I will *never* forgive you for the time that you slept with her in our bed when I was out of town."

Rosa forgave Sam 90 percent and that was enough for them to move forward in their marriage. Sam had worked hard over time to earn her forgiveness and rebuild trust. In certain ways their marriage was stronger than ever. I suspect Sam respected his wife more for continuing to claim her 10 percent. Maybe, over many years, the 10 percent of nonforgiveness would lessen, or maybe not. In any case, Rosa knew she was on solid ground not to forgive everything.

MY AUNT ANNIE: THE QUEEN OF HOLDING A GRUDGE

In stark contrast to people who rush to a superficial forgiveness, some folks practice radical *non*forgiveness. My aunt Annie, my father's big sister, was one of them. She cut off all contact with me after I did not thank her for a gift she sent me when I was a sophomore at the University of Wisconsin. I made careful efforts as an adult to apologize and to restore some contact but every effort I made over decades was rebuked.

My cards and packages were returned unopened. The two times I attempted to call her at her Los Angeles apartment, she slammed down the phone as soon as she knew it was me. The only correspondence she replied to was my wedding invitation, which she returned with a scathing letter of refusal. She had no contact with my sister, Susan, either. Forgiveness was not her thing. She never let go of an insult, real or imagined.

Cutoff was a time-honored tradition in my father's family. We mammals are wired for fight or flight under stress, and my aunt Annie and others on this side of my family tree were heavily wired for flight. My paternal grandmother, Tillie, had no contact with any living person in her family. At the time of her death, she was not on speaking terms with Annie, her only daughter. They hadn't spoken for almost twenty years, although they lived in the same neighborhood.

Both my father and mother were children of Russian Jewish immigrant parents who faced immeasurable hardships and losses, including the traumatic emigration from the old country. In my mother's family "blood was thicker than water," and the more difficult the circumstances, the more this close-knit immigrant family drew together.

But my father's family managed the anxious aftermath of the emigration and loss in a very different manner. Anyone who got mad would quickly disconnect from the relationship, as if they had gone back to the old country, never to return. If you fought with a family member or offended him, that person might never forgive you or even recognize your existence. It took me a long time to truly accept that there was nothing I could ever do or say that would make my aunt Annie speak to me. It was ineffably sad, even though I knew better than to take it personally.

Every family and culture has its own traditions

about offering and accepting the olive branch. Family therapist Monica McGoldrick has written about the Irish tradition of nonforgiveness, quoting a joke about Irish Alzheimer's ("You forget everything except the grudges"). In contrast, Jewish culture places a great emphasis on forgiveness.

As with all generalizations, there are countless exceptions to the rule. My relatives on my father's side included the kings and queens of cutoff. Monica, who is firmly grounded in her Irish roots, is profoundly openhearted and dedicated to helping people stay connected in the face of profound differences. Her book *You Can Go Home Again* inspires readers to view difficult family members through the widest, most compassionate lens. My aunt Annie would have thrown the book in the garbage.

It's useful to consider how members of your own family practice compassion and forgiveness when a hurt has not been repaired. Thinking about family patterns can help you see your own habitual way of responding to insults and injuries more clearly. Few would choose to take my aunt Annie to be a role model. Nor do we necessarily want to hold hands with all the people who hurt us and sing "Kumbaya." As with most things, the extremes are not useful.

ONE TRUE THING

I've worked with people over many decades who are struggling with the forgiveness question and I know this one thing to be true: You do not need to forgive a person who has hurt you in order to free yourself from the pain of negative emotions. You can even reach a place of love and compassion for the wrongdoer without forgiving a particular action or inaction. You are not a less loving or whole person if there are certain things you do not forgive, and certain people whom you choose not to see. Perhaps you are even a stronger or more courageous person if you have leftover anger, whether from one violation or countless little microviolations, even as you move on.

Most importantly, it is no one else's job—not that of your therapist, mother, teacher, spiritual guide, best friend, or relationship expert—to tell you to forgive—or not to.

CHAPTER 11

How to Find Peace

The more the wrongdoer seems untouched by his bad deeds, the more he appears to be going merrily on his way, the more tightly the hurt party may cling to anger, bitterness, and pain. When there has been no heartfelt apology, remorse, or acknowledgment on the part of the person who has injured us, what then? What keeps us mired in our suffering and what releases us from it?

We all want to suffer less, yet we may reflexively lock ourselves into ways of thinking that block us from resolution and letting go. Our longing for justice, the singularly human struggle to make sense of the other person's behavior, and our tendency to take things personally, are among the factors that may keep us from moving on—whether from a small insult by a stranger, or from a devastating betrayal in an important relationship.

MY MOTHER'S BEST ADVICE (EASIER SAID THAN DONE)

When I was a little girl growing up in Brooklyn, I learned a lesson of great value from my mother. If someone said or did something unkind (a nasty person at the supermarket checkout counter, for example) my mother would say, "She must be a very unhappy person." She didn't say this to make excuses; it was simply a calm observation that I translated into this advice: "Don't take things quite so personally; unhappiness or insecurity can make people say stupid things. When other people act badly, it has to do with them, not with you."

My mother's words helped me to be less reactive, to pass on less intensity than I receive, to see people as more complex than their worst behaviors, to develop empathy, and to be curious about why people do what they do. It's a perspective that serves me well in my work as a psychotherapist. Away from my consulting room, however, I do not always operate at this high level of maturity.

Checking In at My Doctor's Surgery

I'm reminded of a recent interaction at a doctor's surgery. I was a new patient waiting in line to be checked in by a young receptionist whom I noted was very personable. She greeted everyone warmly and was all smiles and good cheer as she copied people's insurance cards and gave them the usual forms to fill out.

Until she came to me, that is. At once her demeanor changed. She wouldn't look at me, and her voice sounded so clipped and cold that I wondered if maybe I had some doppelgänger out there who was running around stalking her or taking the air out of her tires. I felt pulled down as I ruminated about why this young woman had taken such an obvious and immediate dislike to me.

I also felt angry at her for her rudeness. I wanted to pointedly ask, "Have I done anything to offend you?" and also, "Are you aware that some of the people you're checking in have serious medical issues and are scared to death about test results, and does it occur to you that maybe you should be nice to *all* of these people, and that includes me?" Of course, I had the good sense to suck it up.

About an hour later I happened to be in the medical office parking lot. It was lunchtime, and there appeared this same young woman walking toward her car. She spotted me and darted right over. I was certain she was going to apologize, as I thought she should, although actually I would have preferred not to see her at all.

"Oh, Dr. Lerner," she said, this time looking down at her feet. "I just want to tell you how much your books have meant to me. I read *The Dance of Anger* last year, and it changed my life. When I saw you in the office I got so nervous I couldn't even speak. I must have looked like an idiot. I just want to say that it's an honor to meet you."

"Well, it's an honor to meet you, too," I said. We shook hands and she went back to her car. I thought to myself, "There's definitely a lesson or two here."

The lesson is obviously not that everyone who appears rude is actually a secret fan. Rather, my story brings home the fact that we misread people's motives all the time, and in the absence of facts, we are left with our fantasies (Had she heard something bad about me? Was it my torn jeans?) or ruminations ("Why are people so senselessly mean when life is already hard enough?"). We engage in mind-reading, which, in contrast to intuition, humans have no talent for.

"I JUST WANT TO UNDERSTAND!"

Where there has been no apology and no way to make sense of an injury, the hurt party often tells me:

> *"I just need to understand how he could have done this to me. Then I could let it go."*

> *"What was going on in her mind? How can she live with herself? Does she even think about it?"*

> *"How can someone who loves me behave this way?"*

How do we explain the inexplicable? Not simply the rudeness of strangers, but the hurtful actions of the very people who were supposed to nurture and protect us. Why did they leave us so totally alone, fail to protect or rescue us, or otherwise behave very badly? This is a puzzle that a child may struggle with even before she has the words to articulate it. "Is it because I am too good or too bad, too pretty or too ugly, too special or too worthless, too needy or too unable to fix my parent's need?"

Children seek meaning for the hurtful behavior of family members very early on, often relying on self-blaming fantasies that serve to preserve their image of the "good parent" on whom they utterly depend. Children have a strong sense of justice combined with an equally strong wish to forgive those they depend on and love.

In our adult relationships, we may still be struggling with this same question. "Why would someone who loves me behave this way?" We may replay a version of our painful past, for example, by our poor choice of friends or partners. It's not that we have a masochistic wish to repeat history. Instead, we may be attempting to heal the past, by changing *this* person through the power of our love, goodness, suffering, or saintlike patience and tolerance. Perhaps if we try hard enough we can give an old story a different ending. Or, if not that, perhaps we can figure out at last what makes a wrongdoer tick, or so the fantasy goes.

"MY MOTHER IS BORDERLINE"

These days, people often try to make sense of the most difficult people in their lives by diagnosing them. I can't count the number of men and women I've worked with who come bounding into my office, buoyed by a discovery that offers them obvious relief. They show me the book they're reading in which they have found a family member on every page. Their mother is *borderline*. Their sister has a *narcissistic personality disorder*.

These labels offer some real comfort. Formal diagnoses can help the hurt party shed whatever sense of responsibility they may still carry for "causing" a family member's inexplicable behavior or for failing to fix it. Diagnostic labels can also provide a sense of community. What went on in your house while you were growing up is not a shameful and isolating story—countless others had or have parents or siblings with these same diagnoses.

The hurt party may view the diagnostic label as explaining and even justifying a family member's hurtful behaviors, the way a brain tumor might explain a sudden aggressive outburst. In truth, most of these labels neither excuse nor explain much of anything. They are not the lens through which I view human emotional functioning, and I believe the majority of psychiatric diagnoses do more harm than good.

Still, I have come to understand that giving a formal psychiatric diagnosis to the offending party does seem to lessen the suffering of hurt individuals. "*That's why she did it! She has an official mental disorder.*" There's some vulgar truth to the quip, "Sometimes the first step toward forgiveness is realizing the other person is totally bat-shit crazy."

Of far greater value than diagnosing and labeling people is knowing their history and their stories, and having a solid theory about how anxiety and shame can drive good people to do bad things. My work as a psychologist centers on helping people gain a broader view and more objective understanding of family members, which includes recognizing their strengths and their vulnerabilities. We all have both.

Knowing the facts of family history over generations, achieving a wider historical perspective, and understanding the patterns and triangles in which we all participate, can change the meaning of a family member's behavior. As we pull back and widen the lens setting, we temper our anger with compassion, even as we hold that person accountable for their actions. It always helps to have a larger picture, even when we choose not to forgive.

BALANCING THE SCALES OF JUSTICE

The wish to make sense of the wrongdoer is only part of the picture. The hurt party who says, "I just want to understand!" may also want the unrepentant wrongdoer to suffer the way he has made her suffer—a perfectly normal human impulse.

"I'm innocent, and I'm the one who's suffering," a therapy client, Amanda, tells me. Her fiancée,

Meghan, had broken off their engagement without warning some two years before Amanda sought my help. They had waited for a long time for the legal right to marry, the "save the date" invitations had been sent out, and wedding plans were under way. Her fiancée explained her departure with empty clichés ("I love you but I'm not in love with you"; "You deserve better than me"), then made herself unavailable for more conversation. Of course, Amanda wants to see her punished, if not in this life, then in the next one. Her ex-partner quickly moved on to a new relationship, without ever looking back.

Losses we don't see coming are the most difficult to deal with. And sometimes the hardest part of a painful ordeal is that the wrongdoer doesn't seem to suffer at all. When Amanda sought my help two years after the breakup, she still couldn't stop ruminating about it. Not all the time, of course, but one thing or another would evoke the past, and there it would be all over again, the clenched heart, the depressed feeling, the intense rage.

When the non-apologetic wrongdoer has never been accountable, our reactive brain excels in rehashing grievances ("How could my ex do this to the children?"). Our anger may be totally legitimate, but rather than leading to productive problem-solving, it just digs a big negative groove in our brain and disrupts our sleep. If, however, we soften our hearts toward the target of our resentment or hatred, or start letting the anger recede into the background, we may be confronted by a new set of challenges that we don't anticipate. Sometimes it's easier to cling to old resentments, and continue to carry their full weight, than to put down the heavy load of resentment and hurt.

"LOOK WHAT YOU'VE DONE TO ME!"

Sometimes we are just not ready to detach from our anger. It's not that we take some twisted pleasure in feeling like the done-in partner, although we may have grown accustomed over time to wrapping pain and suffering around ourselves like an old, familiar blanket. More importantly, staying angry and "done in" can serve us, without our conscious awareness or intent, in the following four ways.

First, our suffering can be our way of taking revenge, by showing the other person as well as the world how deeply his or her behavior has harmed us. To move forward in our lives, to really get back on our feet, may feel akin to forgiving the one who injured us, as if we were saying: "Okay, I'm doing pretty well now, so I guess your behavior didn't really hurt me *that* much."

Second, the anger we allow ourselves to feel toward one offending individual can serve to protect a different and more important relationship. You can't forgive your daughter-in-law's rudeness, which allows you to avoid experiencing any anger at your own son's passivity, as he takes no responsibility for how you are treated by his wife. You have never felt the anger at your father's long-time demeaning and arrogant behaviors, but then you cut off contact with your brother because he failed to come to Dad's funeral. You blame your alcoholic ex-wife for the irresponsible ways she behaved when your children were in her care post-divorce, because it protects you from experiencing your own shame for failing to protect your kids, knowing as you did that your ex was not competent to take care of them. We're unlikely to let go of a negative focus on one person if it allows us to protect our favored image of a different person or relationship, including our relationship with our own self.

The third reason we may resist letting go of our anger is that it keeps us connected to the very person who has hurt us. Anger is a form of intense (albeit negative) attachment just like love. Both anger and love keep us close to the other person, which is why so many couples are *legally* divorced, but not *emotionally* divorced. If, many years post-separation, you still can't talk on the phone or be in the same room with your ex-spouse without feeling your stomach clutch, then you're still attached.

Finally, clinging to an angry internal dialogue keeps the fantasy of obtaining justice alive—that one magical day when the offender will have a *Eureka!* experience and see what he's done. No one makes a plan to cling to a connection that gives the offender so much power over our current emotional life. Yet, as Katrina's story illustrates, it is so hard to let go of this hope.

WHY YOU CAN'T STOP HATING YOUR EX

I saw Katrina in consultation three times when I was conducting a workshop for therapists in Los Angeles. This is her story as she told it to me.

Katrina was married for fifteen years to a man who left her after becoming hugely successful in the tech world. She told me she had provided unflagging love and consistent support for his work, sacrificing career opportunities of her own to raise their daughter while he put all of his time and energy into his start-up company. When he insisted three years before she sought my help that they move from Chicago to Los Angeles for an even more prestigious and lucrative position, she reluctantly agreed.

Eight months after the move, he filed for divorce and moved in with a marketing director of a large advertising firm, a young, beautiful, and self-made millionaire in her own right. Katrina subsequently learned that the move to L.A. was motivated by a five-year long-distance affair; that is, he had it all planned out. When he filed for divorce, he hired one of the city's most powerful and aggressive attorneys, and she ended up signing a settlement agreement that left her with far less money than she was due.

Their ten-year-old daughter, Ana, now adored the new girlfriend and preferred staying in their home in the Hollywood Hills that had a swimming pool and big entertainment center. The girlfriend bought Ana a puppy that she loved, and Ana told Katrina that she didn't like being away from her dog. Katrina described layer upon layer of pain.

Katrina hated everything about L.A. Because of their daughter, she felt moving back to Chicago where she had friends and a sister wasn't an option. She requested the consultation with me because she wanted some direction in how to let go of her intense anger and hatred toward her ex. She now had a good job and several new friends, but every time she thought about her ex—his beautiful and successful partner, the tremendous prestige of the couple, their fancy home where her daughter preferred to hang out, the many levels of deception that included his plotting out the move—her rage erupted full-force.

Katrina told me that she wanted to find some way to "forgive him and move on" but could not, for a particular reason. In her words, "I feel violated and beaten to a pulp. The hardest thing is that I have no forum to show the world what he did to me." She paused and added, "This may sound crazy, but I wish he had actually beaten me. I wish I had the physical bruises that would allow me to bring him to justice."

If only it had happened *that* way, she explained, with physical evidence that could be substantiated, she could take it to court, and there, in front of lawyers, judges, and the men and women of the jury, she could tell her story. Everyone would see what he had done. His shark of a lawyer would lose the case.

This fantasy, this courtroom, was now where she lived. Here she would be heard and believed. Her husband would be forced to face his cruelty, her pain, and the extent that he had violated, deceived, and tricked her. He would go to jail, his reputation ruined, and there would be justice and reparation. He would no longer be able to fool his friends, their daughter, himself. The courtroom scene was so vivid to her, so repeatedly rehearsed, she could see the smallest details of the majestic room, the faces of the sympathetic and shocked members of the jury, her ex-husband covering his head in shame as he faced the photographers from the *Los Angeles Times,* where the story would appear. It was the stuff movies are made of, the unexpected and satisfying ending where truth and justice prevail. She replayed the scene endlessly in her mind.

But the courtroom scene, while offering momentary comfort each time she replayed it, also provided the glue that fastened her to the false beliefs that did not serve her—that her ex needed to see what he had done to her and that subsequently she needed to forgive him. These were the keys that she thought would unlock the door of the small, unhappy place that imprisoned her. Instead, they helped keep her trapped.

"I can't forgive him until I can make him see the situation he has put me in and what he's done to me." I've heard these words from countless men and women post-divorce who, with good reason, feel stuck in the role of the done-in partner, especially if there were not other significant people to witness and validate what occurred.

My Feedback

Katrina wanted any ideas I had about how she could get her ex to see the truth of what he had done. Maybe, with the right words in a letter, or by making him sit down and listen to her feelings one more time, or by confronting the new partner, or even by publishing a short memoir or an op-ed piece in the paper, she might make him see what he had put her through, and then she might be able to finally forgive him. To her enormous credit, she had not gone the usual route of trying to enlist Ana into her camp at the expense of Ana's relationship with her dad. This was a remarkable achievement.

Katrina deserved a medal of honor for staying ambulatory and breathing, for putting her clothes on every day and going to work, and for taking good care of her daughter. Given the multiple losses and deceptions she experienced, of course she felt profoundly done-in. I told her that her longing for witnesses, and for the unequivocal validation of her feelings, were totally normal. And for all of us, current hurts and obfuscations of our reality gain additional power from the inevitable unrepaired and unacknowledged injuries of childhood.

I also told Katrina what she did not want to hear—that her ex would never see what he had done to her and make amends. There was no expert, myself included, who could ever make him see the truth, or feel guilty, or feel anything at all. She could run the courtroom scene through her mind as long as she needed to, for the rest of her life if she chose to. The unequivocal and heartfelt validation she deserved would not come from him. Nor did she need to forgive his actions to free herself from the pain of what he had done.

Two Years Later

I referred Katrina to a therapist in her area who I knew was a skilled and empathic listener and also an expert in EMDR (Eye Movement Desensitization and Reprocessing), a relatively efficient treatment that, when it works, can lighten the emotional impact of trauma and offer considerable relief.

I heard from Katrina by email several years later. She was doing a lot better. The steady, clear, and direct validation the therapist provided was a part of the healing. The EMDR helped her to feel lighter and keep the painful feelings more at a distance. The therapist had also recommended medication to help soothe her overheated nervous system and give her some relief from the kind of obsessive thinking that she knew didn't serve her well. She was now running, eating healthily, getting sunshine and sleep, and taking care of herself. All these things, plus time, helped.

Katrina also shared her experience attending a two-day forgiveness workshop. Because forgiveness was still something she sought, it was a wise investment of her time and money. The workshop leader honored the ongoing presence of the participants' anger and resentment, and had developed seven forgiveness exercises that included, among other things, enveloping the offender in white light, while sending him compassion, benevolence, and love.

Katrina told me that she "flunked the forgiveness part," and added that perhaps forgiveness wasn't her talent. But during the workshop she had several insights, well worth the price of admission, that stayed with her.

First, she realized that relationships are not some kind of competition where the one who gets out first, or with most of the goods, is the winner. She also realized that at some level her husband could not be as happy as he appeared or even believed himself to be, because people who deceive and diminish others are not deeply happy and fully at peace with themselves. Finally, she realized that despite some ongoing envy and resentment for the "good life" he had, she did not want to *be* him. She did not want to be a person who would do what he had done. Her dignity and integrity were intact, qualities far more important than what money could buy.

Katrina said that these were not new insights for her, but often what we need most to learn is not new. Rather, we most need to learn what we already know and to know and live it at a deeper level.

NO SIX EASY STEPS

I don't mean to imply that we hold on to our anger simply because we unconsciously want to show the other person how totally they've screwed up our lives, or because it maintains our connection to them, or because it lets us keep alive the fantasy that one day that person will change the way we want them to. Nor are these feelings completely in our control. We don't just decide one day, "Gee, I think this would be a good time to let go of my anger and suffering."

Countless self-help books, blogs, and seminars promise relief from suffering, when pain and suffering are as much a part of life as happiness and joy. The only way to avoid being mistreated in this world is to fold up in a dark corner and stay mute. If you go outside, or let others in, you'll get hurt many times. Ditto if you've grown up in a family rather than being raised by wolves. Some people will behave badly and will not apologize, repair the harm, or care about your feelings.

There are countless resources out there to aid us with the process of letting go, when we have the will and intention to move in this direction. Therapy, meditations, medication, yoga, religious and spiritual practices, exercise, writing and making art, breathing and relaxation exercises, and being useful to others, are just a few of the available paths and concrete strategies to help us stop nursing past grievances and live more peacefully in the present.

How do you find peace when the hurt you've suffered will never be acknowledged or repaired by the one who inflicted it? The answer is as simple as the challenge is daunting. *Any way you can.* It's worthwhile finding a concrete strategy, healing practice, or larger perspective that suits you, or a new way of thinking that speaks to you. While you're ruminating about the terrible things your ex (or mother or Uncle Charlie) did to you, and making yourself miserable in the process, the person who has hurt you may be having a fabulous day at the beach. This is as good a reason as any to make use of the resources that are out there to help you grab a bit more peace of mind.

The hardest part is that it requires us to accept that the offending party is never going to apologize, never going to see himself or herself objectively, never going to listen to our feelings with the slightest openness of mind or heart. Letting go of anger and hate requires us to give up the hope for a different past, along with the hope of a fantasized future. What we gain is a life more in the present, where we are not mired in prolonged anger and resentment that doesn't serve us.

CHAPTER 12

The Two Most
Powerful Words in the
English Language

"I'm sorry" are the two most healing words in the English language. When they are spoken as part of a wholehearted apology, these words are the greatest gift we can give to the person we have offended. Our apology can help free the hurt person from life-draining anger, bitterness, and pain. It validates their sense of reality by affirming that, yes, their feelings make sense, we get it, and we take full responsibility for our words and actions (or our failure to speak or act). A heartfelt apology allows the hurt party the space to explore the possibilities of healing instead of just struggling to make sense of it all.

The apology is also a gift to our self. Our self-respect and level of maturity rest squarely on our ability to see ourselves objectively, to take a clear-eyed look at the ways that our behavior affects others, and to acknowledge when we've acted at another person's expense. The good apology also earns us respect in the eyes of others, even though we may fear the opposite.

Finally, the good apology is a gift to the relationship. Two people can feel secure in the knowledge that if they behave badly, even fight terribly, they can repair the disconnection. We strengthen our relationships when others know that we're capable of reflecting on our behavior, and that we'll listen to their feelings and do our best to set things right.

THE TRAGEDY OF A FAILED APOLOGY

In contrast to the profoundly healing power of the good apology, there is the terrific cost of a failed apology—a "Sorry Not Sorry," in the current Internet parlance. Consider this example of the high stakes of an apology gone wrong.

Suzanne, a Texan in her thirties, requested a phone consultation with me because her younger sister Marietta hadn't spoken to her in almost a year. She feared they might be heading for a lifelong cutoff. Since cutoff was a family tradition over generations, the stakes were high.

Here's what happened as Suzanne told it: The night of their mother's funeral service the previous year, Suzanne had too much to drink and said some cruel things to Marietta. Her angry words were fueled by grief, and by her accumulated anger that Marietta, who lived across the country, had done almost none of the caretaking for their mother.

On the fateful night in question, Suzanne accused her sister of never having loved their mother, and of caring only about the inheritance, and when she woke up the next morning she felt so ashamed that she couldn't bring herself to apologize. So all she said to her sister about the night before was, "I think I had too much to drink."

After Suzanne returned home and realized that Marietta was barely speaking to her, she offered numerous belated apologies. Marietta, however, didn't respond to her bids for connection. Faced with being stonewalled, Suzanne began to feel like *she* was the victim. She now blamed Marietta for being rigid and unforgiving.

As I questioned Suzanne about the specifics of her apologies, it was clear to me why her fence-mending efforts were going nowhere. At first, Suzanne had said nothing to her sister after insulting her. Later she offered endless *sorrys* that were emptied of all accountability for her hurtful accusations.

Suzanne's *sorrys* went like this:

"I said some terrible things that night. I am so sorry that you had to hear them."

"I'm so sorry that you felt so hurt. You know how much I love you."

"I am so sorry that what I said seems to have ruined our relationship."

"Please forgive me. I'm sorry that when I drink too much I say things I shouldn't."

What was wrong with Suzanne's apologies? Well, everything. Her tearful apologies were full of emotion, but empty of personal responsibility. She never offered a direct, unequivocal expression of guilt, remorse, and regret for the words she had spoken. She didn't get down on her proverbial knees the morning after to offer one true apology that might have gone something like this:

> *"Marietta, I have no words to express how sorry I am that I said hurtful, outrageous things that I do not believe. I don't expect you to forgive me and right now I can't forgive myself. I only want you to know that in the light of day, I do not believe any of those things. I can only promise you that I will never again say such hurtful and untrue words or attack you out of my own anxiety and grief. There is no excuse for what I said."*

As a result of our telephone consultation, Suzanne decided to send a handwritten card to her sister that took unambiguous responsibility and expressed heartfelt remorse for her hurtful words and for her earlier failed apologies. Suzanne's written apology—her first genuine statement of accountability since their mother's death—was important to offer, whether Marietta accepted it or not. Suzanne would ultimately feel better for having done the right thing, regardless of how Marietta responded.

Part of the vulnerability of apologizing is that we have no control over how the other person will respond. The apology is a leap into the unknown. The last I heard, the two sisters were back on speaking terms, although their relationship was still strained and distant. In my professional work I am struck by how often sibling relationships fall apart around the life-cycle stage of caring for elderly parents, and dealing with a parent's death and its aftermath. Failed apologies have the most serious consequences at stressful points in the life cycle, and loss is the most challenging adaptational task that family members have to come to terms with.

I hope that Suzanne can follow her good apology with further healing conversations, and resist falling back into a defensive, muddled mode. I also hope that Marietta can soften up. A sister relationship is a big thing to lose. Nor can we orphan ourselves from our first family. When we cut off from a close family member, that person becomes an even bigger presence inside us.

TWO APOLOGIES

I would like to conclude this book by sharing two very different apologies. The first is a short apology involving a stolen bicycle. The second is an apology I gave to a dear friend—one that was as difficult as it was essential.

Apology #1: "Sorry I Stole Your Bike!": A Onetime Apology Between Strangers

My friend Rick recently had his bike stolen from his garage in downtown Lawrence, Kansas. This was a big bummer but, unlike the story of most bike thefts, it had a happy ending. In an email, Rick described the event to me as follows:

> At around four in the morning I woke up in a funk as I couldn't believe someone had stolen my bike right before I was leaving on vacation. I went out-side hoping against all hope that the bike would be back in the garage. It was not. But then I looked in the driveway and there it was—in all of its stolen beauty! It was the answer to my prayers.
>
> More surprising still was the simple handwritten note taped to the bike. It appeared to be written by someone who had little formal education. It read, "*I apologize so much for taking your bike. I was drunk and dumb. And I am sorry that I don't have the courage to tell you in person.*" I was touched by this sincere expression of responsibility and remorse offered to my friend. While it says, "I was drunk and dumb," it doesn't slide into, "The bottle made me do it."

The author of this note wasn't hoping for a restored relationship, since there was none to begin with. Nor was he hanging around to get a smile or pat on the back from the bike's owner. He gained nothing tangible from his apology—in fact, there was a certain risk to his returning to the scene of the crime to give back stolen property.

We don't need to be experts in the apology business to recognize when "I'm sorry" comes from the heart and from a simple wish to do the right thing. I was touched by the note, which reminded me that sometimes the only motive behind an apology is the wish to restore one's integrity, to heal the relationship with one's own self.

Apology #2: Letting Go of My Need to Be Right

Sheila, a close friend of many decades, invited me to her book party in New York. It was scheduled at a difficult time for me to leave Kansas and the plane tickets were expensive. Still, I wanted to be there for her. I've learned how important it is to show up for rituals, and the launching of Sheila's first book was a huge event for her.

I arrived at the party to find I knew only one other person besides Sheila, a woman named Blanche, who was the senior editor of a magazine where I had been a columnist for many years. I ended up sitting in a corner with Blanche for almost two hours, lost in a conversation, and oblivious to the passage of time. Neither of us noticed when the guests began to gather in a different room to offer toasts, so we joined the group midway through the ritual.

When Sheila called me the evening after I returned home, I assumed she was going to thank me for making the trip, but instead she told me I had behaved incomprehensibly (or was the word *reprehensibly?*) at her party. She went on to share how hurt (and furious) she was. How could I have sat with one person for almost the entire party, making no effort to circulate and meet her friends? Didn't I know that many of her guests had read my books, and had been eager to meet me? And how could I have been so self-absorbed that I missed half of the ritual taking place in the other room? I had disappointed her friends and embarrassed her.

I felt blindsided. I'd had no idea there had been a problem at all. I had made an expensive trip at an inconvenient time to be at the book party, and now I was being told that I had ruined it. Her criticisms seemed exaggerated and unfair, so I responded in defensive mode with, "*I'm sorry, but . . .*"

"I'm sorry," I said, "but why in the world didn't you pull me away from Blanche early on and let me know what you wanted?"

"That's not my responsibility," Sheila fired back at me.

"I'm not saying it's your responsibility," I answered. "I'm just saying that of course I would have circulated if you had asked me to. A tap on the shoulder would have done it."

"It's not my job to supervise you or tell you how to behave." Sheila was even angrier than before. I had obviously thrown fuel on the fire.

I was really upset. Why couldn't Sheila see that we had *both* participated in the problem? It would have been the easiest thing in the world for her to tell me she'd like to introduce me to some of her friends. And of course, I would have wanted to be present at the beginning of the toasts if I had but known they were starting. Instead of doing the mature thing, Sheila had stayed silently seething for much of the party, as if she were the helpless victim of my gross insensitivity, for which she then blamed me. The fact that I had come to New York at considerable trouble and expense grated. The fact that she couldn't see her part grated more. I ended the conversation with another classic faux-apology: "*I'm really sorry you were so upset by my talking so long to Blanche.*"

Over the next couple of days, away from the heat of anger, I took stock of my defensiveness. Sheila had gathered the courage to confront me about *my* behavior. She wanted me to hear her criticisms, which was not the time for me to criticize her back. She had made herself vulnerable by sharing her anger and deep hurt. Whether I saw these feelings as completely "valid" or not was irrelevant. They were her feelings.

I often feel a great need to get my close friends to see how they should have handled a situation differently, whether with me or with someone else. I recognize this as a problem of mine—the downside of my clarity about relationship patterns. Sheila has many wonderful qualities, but one she does not have is the ability to see her part in the interactions that bring her pain. My response on the phone could only have felt to her like I was trying to reverse the blame, which I was. At the very least, I wanted her to share it.

I called Sheila a few days later and offered a genuine apology. I asked her more about her feelings and about the disappointment of her friends who had wanted to meet me. I told her I was sorry for causing such hurt, and especially at such an important occasion. I said I had given her words much thought and that there was no excuse for sitting in the corner with one person for so long—a decidedly thoughtless act. I meant it all. It was her book party, her very big night. I had screwed up.

Yes, I secretly wished she could have said, "Well, Harriet, it's also true that I should have said something, so I share at least a teensy bit of the responsibility." I let this hope go. A true apology focuses exclusively on the hurt feelings of the other person, and not on what we would like to get for ourselves, like forgiveness, or, in my case, Sheila's recognition of her part in the bigger picture.

BE GENEROUS

I'm not suggesting that you give in to unreasonable demands when doing so is too much at your expense. Nor am I suggesting that you apologize for things you're not responsible for. Rather, I'm suggesting that you tend generously to the vulnerability of others. People enter close relationships with a deep longing that the other person will tend to their wounds and not throw salt on them. Don't we hope for this in all our significant relationships?

A wholehearted apology means valuing the relationship, and accepting responsibility for our part without a hint of evasion, excuse-making, or blaming. Sometimes the process is less about insisting on justice and more about investing in the relationship and the other person's happiness. It's about accepting the people you love as they are, as I did with Sheila, and having the maturity to apologize for our part even when the other person's feelings seem exaggerated, or they can't see their own contribution to the problem.

Lead with your heart and not your attack dog. It's difficult and it's worth it. The courage to apologize, and the wisdom and clarity to do so wisely and well, is at the heart of effective leadership, coupledom, parenting, friendship, personal integrity, and what we call love. It's hard to imagine what matters more than that.

Acknowledgments

For careful editing, unflagging support, and invaluable conversation, I am grateful to Marcia Cebulska, Jeffrey Ann Goudie, Emily Kofron, and Caryn Mirriam-Goldberg. I can't imagine the writing life without them nearby.

For improving select parts of the manuscript and responding to my calls for help along the way, thanks to Marianne Ault-Riché, Shirley Bonney, Doris Jane Chediak, Julie Cisz, Ann Cobb, Debbie Frederick, Robert McAllister, Rabbi Fred Reiner, Sheila Reynolds, Marian Sandmaier, Rabbi Debbie Stiel, and Stephanie von Hirschberg. I also want to thank Tom Averill, Carolyn Conger, Judie Koontz, Susan Kraus, Alice Lieberman, Libby Rosen, Karen Rowinsky, and Ellen Safier, for their support over decades.

Jo-Lynne Worley has been my manager, agent, and friend since we joined forces in the fall of 1990. Her competence and commitment to my work has been unwavering and sustaining. Jo-Lynne's partner in work and love, Joanie Shoemaker, has also offered her friendship and invaluable editing help throughout the writing of this book.

I'm fortunate that *Why Won't You Apologize?* landed with Touchstone/Simon & Schuster. My editor, Michelle Howry, offered enthusiastic support and vital suggestions, and Lara Blackman did a terrific job stepping in at the last hour during the production stage. Thanks also go to Tara Parsons, Anne Jones, Pete Garceau, Cherlynne Li, Linda Sawicki, Kelsey Manning, and Shida Carr for their important contributions. Adding to my good luck has been the honor of working with the remarkable Susan Moldow, president and publisher of Touchstone. Her husband, Bill Shinker, gave me my start in publishing many moons ago when the chances of seeing my work in print looked bleak. I'm not alone in my opinion that Susan and Bill represent the best of the publishing world. Coming to Touchstone feels like coming full circle.

I met my husband, Steve, when we were doctoral students in clinical psychology at CUNY in the late sixties. I have no words to describe how lucky I am to be his comrade in love and work over so many decades. He has lent a gifted editorial hand to all my books, and I thank him for everything.

Our two sons, Matt and Ben, have endured my writing about them when they were little and have become people I now turn to for wise council. Apart from his expertise on all things technological, Matt's clarity on how (and if) to open conversations regarding difficult work-related issues has been immensely helpful. My younger son, Ben, barely out of diapers when I was working on my first book, is now an accomplished writer who offered thoughtful criticisms of this manuscript at various stages. I'm enormously proud of both of my sons. It is to them, and their remarkable wives and children, that this book is dedicated.

My gratitude extends across long distances to my enthusiastic readers who continue to share their warm and generous responses to my work, reminding me during the inevitable low points in authorhood that it's all worthwhile. My therapy clients have entrusted me with their stories since the start of my career and continue to inspire me with their courage. Without them, there would be no books.

Finally, I owe a great debt to Brené Brown, whose regard for my work and generosity of spirit continue to bring countless new readers on board. Her own contributions as researcher, writer, and storyteller are boundless. On the challenge of forgiveness and rebuilding trust when "I'm sorry" is not enough, Janis Abrahms Spring's books are essential. On the subject of effective apologies, I consider the works of Aaron Lazare and John Kador to be classic, and I'm grateful to the eagle-eyed "SorryWatchers" Susan McCarthy and Marjorie Ingall for their online contributions to the discussion.

It is impossible to adequately convey my deep appreciation to those people, too numerous to name individually, who, over the decades, have enriched my thinking, encouraged my writing, and given generously of time they did not have. I am lucky to be blessed with friends, family, and colleagues who are living proof of the old adage, "If you want something done, ask a busy person." I am grateful to have more people to thank than I can ever begin to acknowledge.

Notes

CHAPTER 1

1 Reference to *New Yorker* cartoon, by Zach Kanin.

CHAPTERS 2 AND 3

13 On the subject of the good and bad apology, that covers the public and political sphere, see *On Apology* by Aaron Lazare and *Effective Apology* by John Kador. Also see SorryWatch. com and @SorryWatch on Twitter by Susan McCarthy and Marjorie Ingall.

26 Maggie Nelson, *The Argonauts* (Minnesota: Graywolf Press, 2015), p. 98.

32 Carol Tavris and Elliot Aronson, *Mistakes Were Made (but Not by Me)* (New York: Mariner Books, 2015).

33 Gary Chapman and Jennifer Thomas, *The Five Languages of Apology* (Chicago: Northfield Publishing, 2006).

CHAPTER 4

36 The story of Katherine and Dee first appeared in: *The Dance of Connection* (New York: Harper-Collins, 2002).

CHAPTER 5

53 On *over*-apologizing in the public sphere of Korean life, see: Ed Park, "Sorry Not Sorry," *The New Yorker*, October 19, 2015.

62 On letting go of perfectionism, see Brené Brown's work, including: *The Gifts of Imperfection* (Minnesota: Hazelden, 2010).

63 "While guilt is about *doing*, shame is about *being*." Helen Block Lewis made this distinction in her classic text *Shame and Guilt in Neurosis* (Connecticut: International Universities Press, 1971). Recent popular books on the challenge of overcoming shame include *The Dance of Fear* and *The Dance of Connection*, and Brené Brown's *Rising Strong, Daring Greatly*, and *The Gifts of Imperfection*.

67 On enlarging the offender's platform of self-worth and inviting the wrongdoer to accept responsibility, I am grateful for conversations with friend and colleague Julie Cisz; the writing of Alan Jenkins, including *Invitations to Responsibility*; and the work of Rhea Almeida and her colleagues. My work on how shame blocks the

wrongdoer's capacity to take responsibility first appeared in *The Dance of Connection.*

CHAPTER 6

91 Ellen Wachtel, *We Love Each Other, But* . . . (New York: St. Martin's Press, 1999), p. 85.

CHAPTER 8

109 On courageous acts of change in key relationships, see *The Dance of Anger* and *The Dance of Intimacy.* All of my books owe a great debt to Murray Bowen's teachings on family systems theory, and to feminist theorists and therapists, including Jean Baker Miller, Marianne Ault-Riché, Monica McGoldrick, and *The Women's Project in Family Therapy* (Betty Carter, Peggy Papp, Olga Silverstein, and Marianne Walters).

119 Ellen Wachtel, *We Love Each Other, But* . . . (New York: St. Martin's Press, 1999), p. 14.

119 Researcher John Gottman has concluded that criticism, contempt, defensiveness, and stonewalling are "the four horsemen of the apocalypse" that can clip-clop into the heart of a marriage and destroy it.

CHAPTER 9

127 The opening to the story of Letty and Kim first appeared in *The Dance of Connection.*

CHAPTER 10

137 Claudia Rankine, *Citizen: An American Lyric* (Minnesota: Graywolf Press, 2014), p. 18.

139 Janis Abrahms Spring with Michael Spring, *How Can I Forgive You?* (New York: William Morrow Paperbacks, 2005).

139 On the decision to *not* forgive, see: Roxanne Gay, "Why I Can't Forgive Dylann Roof," *The New York Times*, June 23, 2015.

141 On the transformative power of forgiveness and unconditional love from a spiritual perspective, see: Carolyn Conger, *Through the Dark Forest* (New York: Plume, 2013), pp. 137–156. Also see the work of Sharon Salzberg, author and teacher of the Buddhist principles of loving-kindness and compassion.

143 Anne Lamott, "Have a Little Faith," *AARP The Magazine*, December 2014/January 2015.

145 Janis Abrahms Spring quote from *How Can I Forgive You?*, p. 3.

148 I'm especially grateful to Julie Cisz for her theoretical clarity regarding the problematic aspects of encouraging forgiveness in the therapeutic process and for her generous help with this chapter.

151 Janis Abrahams Spring with Michael Spring, *After the Affair* (New York: William Morrow, 1997).

151 On "The transfer of vigilance": *How Can I Forgive You?*, pp. 124–125.

155 On Irish families, see: Monica McGoldrick, Joe Giordano, Nydia Garcia-Preto, eds., *Ethnicity & Family Therapy, Third Edition* (New York: The Guilford Press, 2005), pp. 595–616. Also see: Monica McGoldrick, *You Can Go Home Again* (New York: W. W. Norton & Company, 1997).

CHAPTER 11

171 Eye movement desensitization and reprocessing (EMDR) is an integrative psychotherapy that can be effective for the treatment of trauma and for relieving many types of psychological distress.

Also published by Duckworth

Gender Medicine
The Groundbreaking New Science of Gender- and Sex-Related Diagnosis and Treatment

MAREK GLEZERMAN

'Absolutely fascinating… mak[es] you think on a deeper level'
William Leith, *Spectator*

Over millions of years, male and female bodies have developed crucial physiological differences to improve the chances for human survival. In *Gender Medicine*, Professor Marek Glezerman, one of the world's leading experts on this new area of medicine, reveals countless differences between the sexes that are frequently overlooked. Often culturally obsolete with the overturning of traditional gender roles, they are nevertheless very real, and go well beyond the obvious sexual and reproductive variances.

For instance, women are more resistant to infectious diseases than men, but are more likely to suffer from autoimmune diseases; female smokers are at greater risk of developing colon cancer than male smokers; Alzheimer's is expressed differently in men and women; the pain threshold is not the same for men and women; drugs to treat nausea work less well for women, and women are more sensitive to antihistamines; aspirin is more effective in preventing strokes in women, but more effective in preventing heart attacks in men... and there is more.

However, the medical establishment still largely treats men and women as though their needs were identical – and medical research is done predominantly on men, with the results then applied to the treatment of women. It is therefore time for a paradigm change – and such a change is the purpose of *Gender Medicine*.

Hardback, ISBN 9780715651148
£20

What the Luck?

The Surprising Role of Chance in Our Everyday Lives

GARY SMITH

'A delightful addition to the stuff-you-think-you-know-that's-wrong genre, á la *Freakonomics*, *Outliers*, and *The Black Swan*'
Kirkus

FACT

- In Israel, pilot trainees who were praised for doing well subsequently performed worse, while trainees who were shouted at for doing poorly performed better.
- Highly intelligent women tend to marry men who are less intelligent.
- US pupils who get the highest scores in grade three generally get lower scores in grade four.

TRUTH

- It's wrong to conclude that shouting is the more effective tool.
- It's wrong to conclude that women choose men whose intelligence does not intimidate them.
- It's wrong to conclude that schools are failing their pupils.

There's one reason for each of these truths: a concept called 'regression to the mean', which explains how we can be misled by luck in our day-to-day lives.

An insufficient appreciation of luck and chance can wreak all kinds of mischief in sports, education, medicine, business and politics. Perfectly natural random variation can lead us to attach meaning to the meaningless. In *What the Luck?*, statistician Gary Smith explains how an understanding of luck can change the way we understand almost every aspect of our lives... and how it can help us learn to rely less on random chance, and more on truth.

Hardback, ISBN 9780715651612
£16.99